JOURNEY THROUGH LOVE

ACIRFA VALENTINE

authorHOUSE®

AuthorHouse™
1663 Liberty Drive
Bloomington, IN 47403
www.authorhouse.com
Phone: 1 (800) 839-8640

Published by AuthorHouse 12/17/2018

ISBN: 978-1-5462-7259-5 (sc)
ISBN: 978-1-5462-7258-8 (hc)
ISBN: 978-1-5462-7257-1 (e)

Library of Congress Control Number: 2018914783

Print information available on the last page.

Any people depicted in stock imagery provided by Getty Images are models, and such images are being used for illustrative purposes only.
Certain stock imagery © Getty Images.

This book is printed on acid-free paper.

INTRODUCTION

Decision

On the day I decided to write this book,

I questioned myself over and over again on whether or not I had anything worthy to say.

Anything worthy to be read.

My goal was to at least inspire one guy out there to do right by his woman. Through reflections, I realized my wrongs and my fault in all that has happened in my love life.

I wanted to share those wrongs with whoever would be willing to read my story and hope that they too can find some kind of awakening if they too shared those conflicts. From the lessons of my past, I hope to assure some stability within marriages and households faced with the same problems.

Most importantly, I hope to finally preserve the innocence for the woman of tomorrow.

They deserve a fair chance

They deserve the promise of love

They deserve the promise of a happily ever after Loss has been a major part of my journey but so has Love and for that I will forever be grateful. It is not at all easy to choose between yesterday and tomorrow but in time I hope to figure it all out,

To love again as I have loved you

In order to understand my journey through love, you will first have to understand me. The funny thing is, my ex fiancé (Lady J) once told me that very same statement. The moment she said it was the last I had heard those words but it never registered. The words went in one ear and out the other without ever fully processing what I had heard. We as humans can be very selfish beings so, for a woman to state she needs to understand you as a person in order for her to fully understand how to love you!... goes a long way. We are not all the same in spite of what you may have heard. We are uniquely beautiful creatures and therefore we All require a certain kind of approach in the ways that we are loved. Sometimes we ourselves don't quite know what that is. In life you have to go through enough life changing experiences to know and understand who you are and most importantly how you are to be loved.

Love languages are a sure thing that actually exist.

In the many times that I have had the pleasures of Love, whether it was me loving her or her loving me, (I say it in that manor because most often we are Not all on the same level playing field and therefore one may be loving as the other is simply enjoying the moment) But to get back on my point, I have noticed that in each of those woman there had to have been a different approach. Some woman love to be touched such as holding hands or a constant since of caress like running my fingers across her back or her thigh. Some Woman are all about communication and wanted to literally talk everything out. Sex life, her monthly cycle, every single daily calorie intake and the emotional roller coaster she may constantly be on. One of my past loves was very different in not showing how she felt at all. A lack of tenderness, lack of emotions unless she was crying over something that I didn't even think would have affected her do to her lack of expression. One was full of joy and beauty. She saw all that was great in the world and ignored all that was ugly and hateful. If anyone ever deserved the audacity of innocence, it surely was her. Those very experiences have helped mold me emotionally as well as spiritually over the years. I am forever thankful for the journey that is love no matter how painful the stories to come may be. Life doesn't happen by chance and we are all meant to go through something. The person that I am or should I say the person that I have become has a lot to do with the way I was brought up and more importantly, the many things that I've seen in my line of work and in some ways have had to overcome. Growing up, I never had the pleasure of seeing my parents together which in my opinion can surely impact a child's view on the world. However my mother, the warrior that she is, was doing it all alone the entire time while my father was believed to be the savior and the provider. I got to witness my mother struggle, I got to see her nightly cries, I got to see what the stresses of life, bills, rent and minimum wage will do to a person. My 2 older sisters and I grew up in a private boarding school overseas. We grew up privileged in many ways but only to come to America and have all those privileges reversed. I remember the day my mother looked me in the eyes and told me that she would never allow me to have my own room because she never had her own room and asked me just who the hell I thought I was. After years of seeing my mother struggle and the understanding of the kind of man that my father was, after leaving a single woman to provide for three kids on her own. Never have I held a grudge against my mother, never have I held any kind of resentment towards her. She herself was broken and was hurting. Hurt people tend to unknowingly hurt other people. She was then and always will remain my first love. Having heard those words that day did set in motion the idea

From an early age I was determined to be a hard worker and make it on my own. So determined that I left home when I was 16 years old. At the age of 16, I moved in with my cousin D money in upstate NY. D money was one of those guys who knew how to hustle his way through life. Very intelligent guy. The kind of a guy who could take apart an entire computer piece by piece and put it back together in no time at all. Because of my cousin I've driven every luxury car I could think of, because of my cousin I've been in many places around many people some of fame and fortune and some of criminal enterprises. To know right out of the gate the kind of man my cousin was, I immediately got myself a job in construction. Construction money at that time was good too, so good that I was able to purchase my first car. Having lived at my cousin's side, it always came with a sense of worry, never know when the Police would come knocking, never knowing when he would get arrested which happened quite a few times. I moved out eventually and was able to get my own apartment. Affirming my own sense of stability. I made myself a promise to never follow in my cousin's footsteps and I made myself a promise to commit each and every time I give my word weather it's in love, in friendship or in business.

MY DEAR LOVE

Far too many days and nights have passed since we last spoke. Time and time again I maintained my silence in fear of saying the wrong thing but I vow to bite my tongue no more. Your absence has me feeling so lost and no compass could ever help find my way back. My personality has even changed to the point I just clash with all those around me. Those who have done me absolutely no wrongs but genuinely tried to get to know me. Often times I wonder if I've lost it. I've never been this lost before. You were my guide, my shining star, my home. I was never confused or ever had I lost my footing when you were my home. Many mistakes were made on both of our parts but I have forgiven them a long time ago. Our entire relationship was to me a living dream, a designed plan by God himself. To separate us must have been a mistake which is why I waited patiently for God to bring you back to me.

Back in my life..

Back as my wife..

Back to restore my life..

These days, I have been doing much better and the power of written words has allowed or should I say helped me to bare the pain. You, the idea of you believe it or not has been my biggest source of inspiration. Night after night you continue to visit me in my dreams with that amazingly beautiful smile. That smile fills me up with so much warmth and joy, it just sets my heart on a running path. To this day, it always manages to make me feel as if you were right here in my arms. To your smile or even the idea of your smile, I manage to lay my head down every night and smile along with you as I fall asleep. In the mornings when I wake, I always awake with a sense of peace. That feeling of peace I carry with me all through my days. The longer I can manage to hold on to that feeling, the longer I keep you (your presence) with me. My whole life has been a journey to find you, to find your love. Now that I think about it, I don't believe I've ever told you how sorry I am. Sorry you ever had to spend a cold night without my arms wrapped around you keeping you warm. Sorry I ever allowed you the space to feel scared or insecure. From the day I laid eyes on you darling, you have never left my sight. Sorry if my lack of communication forced you away. Sorry for the many senseless fights we had over things we barely remembered the very next day. I'm sorry for the shower complications but it was finally fixed before I moved out. Lastly, I am sorry for allowing my pride to keep me from apologizing in the times that I needed to. I had a pretty hard upbringing and my pride was all I had. Looking back on those days, I surely wished I held you much stronger but now my journey continues with the warmest memories of that love.

Your love…

MY WOMAN

The woman that I desire

I would first consider her looks because in spite of what others have said, a woman's look has always been the very first thing that draws us to them. I purposely say looks as appose to beauty because "Beauty" as they say is in the eye of the beholder. In other words, we all define beauty in different ways but she in herself must be beautiful inside as well as on the outside. It would secondly narrow down to her personality. I want to be marveled by her complexion, aroused by her figure and mesmerized by her smile.

I want to be moved by the grief that compels her,

I want to feel her passion, her compassion.

I want to rejoice in her sense of humor.

When the trials, tribulations, complications and the frustrations of life

Are against us; when they come knocking at our door,

I need to be able to rest my head on her breast and find my peace.

I want, No I need!

For her to understand that we would be all that we have.

To understand that we are all binded by a force of life.

In a sense that we are not simply living for ourselves, not just living for the hell of it or for the moment but a part of something much greater. People tend to give up and walk away from what they deemed to be their loved one far too quickly nowadays.

My woman...

The one that I now desire.

Cannot simply be satisfied with living and getting by on a day to day but to always reach for new heights. Every time I accomplish a goal, I begin to ponder upon the next. That kind of a personality will only keep me wanting and needing her even more. If she too should see those same qualities in me, than only then

Will we really and truly see one another as equals.

THE VERY BEGINNING

Love finds us all at different ages and different stages of our lives. For me it happened in the six grade at a high school in Brooklyn NY and her name was Diana. She had a gap in her teeth but the brightest smile and the biggest set of boobies that I had ever seen on a six grader. As clear as if it was just the other day, I remember how we used to make eye contact throughout the entire class session and just stare at each other from across the room. But one day our teacher for that class was out sick and some of the other girls in the class decided to play truth or dare. That day was the very first time Diana and I ever spoke. Brief as it was, it happened very naturally. The game was cut short before we even had the chance to ask each other any questions due to a substitute teacher walking in for coverage.

(I know exactly what you're thinking, what a bummer)

But it still turned out great because in our brief conversation, I offered to walk her home after school. Her house was only about 15 blocks away from the school. The end of the day came and we met at the back of the school to walk over to her house. When we made it to her doorstep, we exchanged phone numbers. While on her doorstep, we held hands as she thanked me for walking her. The excitement of us holding hands had my heart beating extremely fast. In my head, the battle had already been won because my crush was no longer a fantasy but now a reality. Excited as I was, I literally ran the entire way home because I could not wait to dial her number and talk to her some more.. On that evening, we talked on the phone for hours and every day after that for the entire week. That week, word got around rather quickly that that she and I were a couple. In school,

I walked her to class each period and we always ate lunch at the same table together. Now came Friday afternoon and we made plans for our first date that following Saturday. We came to an agreement that we were going to meet at the mall and maybe see a movie. Overly excited, I told my sisters about my girlfriend and of the upcoming movie date. My sisters were the very best siblings by the way. They looked through my entire wardrobe to find me an outfit. It was not only the first date but I had to look cool and who would know better than my 2 older sisters. Besides I had been hanging out with Diana all week long at school and didn't want to wear the same stuff. Now that I had my clothes picked out, the anticipation kept me up throughout the night. Right before I finally went to bed, I looked out my window and saw it had started to snow.

The next morning when I woke up, outside looked like an avalanche came down to my front door. I'm talking about so much snow the cars were just left in place. Most avenues of transportation were temporarily suspended for the street cleanup and snow plows. However, I was determined to see my girl and I have always been that guy that would do just about anything for the pleasures of the heart. With that unwavering state of mind, I put on my brand new Timberland boots; laced them bad boys up and started walking. I fought my way through those mountains of snow piled up on the sidewalk and made it all the way to her house. (Now brace yourselves and get ready for my first heartbreak). I got to her house and knocked on the door when her mother answered. As the polite young man that my mother raised me to be, I greeted her mother and politely asked if I may speak with Diana. Her mother replied "she is somewhere in the neighborhood playing with her friends". All broken down and torn apart, I walked back outside and as I began walking back to my house, I got two blocks away from her house. I saw her and a couple of her friends playing in the snow. (In my head I thought yes, my luck just changed) With the most excited look on my face, I waved and yelled out her name "Diana!!.", She looked back at me (almost with what I would call a "what do you want" face)and simply replied "hi". She continued playing with her friends as if we never spoken before, as if we didn't have any plans on going to a movie. Much like all six grade relationships, ours was short-lived. We saw each other at school that following Monday morning and I surely ignored her as if we had never met. It may sound petty but much like she did me, I felt it was only right to return the favor. In the six grade my heart breaks really didn't last that long as I wasted no time in mourning and found some comfort in the arms of my new Russian crush Irina. Now Irina was a bit taller than me but it didn't bother me much. Irina had long curly brown hair and a mole on the left corner of her toplip. The mole was kind of cute actually, it made her unique and she had some really nice long legs. Irina and I became inseparable rather quickly. We sat together every lunch period. I was always late to all my classes because I walked her to class every period. I walked her home every day too because she lived about six blocks from the school. Irina's parents worked long late hours so, we had plenty of time to hang out, watch TV and make out for the most part. I remember this one specific day it was pouring rain out and Irina and I were walking to her house from school. Irina wasn't like most girls and she wasn't worried or scared of the rain. She simply took off her shoes, grab my hand and we stroll through the rain as if it was a beautiful sunny day out. We even played tag in the rain that day. I chased her, she chased me and every time we caught each other, we kissed.

That kiss in the rain till this very day has been one of my most memorable kisses of all time. I mean we kiss so deeply that the world disappeared. The cars, the people, even the rain disappeared......Even from an early age, the one thing I knew for certain was that heartbreaks were Inevitable. Irina and I ended up breaking up 2 weeks later when she made friends with a Russian boy named Dimitri. Dimitri was just simply an easier choice for her because their parents lived in the same neighborhood, they were both Russian and Irina's biggest fear was her parents finding out that she was dating a black kid. As a parting gift, I wrote her a poem entitled "My Skin" which I have through the years edited and may continue to edit on this journey of love.

My Skin…

Do you,

Can you

Better yet will you see through the color of my skin

Acirfa Valentine

To see your start as I begin

To see your smile in my grin

To see your crime in my sin

Even your victory in my win

Your kiss in my lips

Your thighs in my grip

Your switch in my hips

Even when you are no longer toned

But now big boned

Will the struggles of life break us

Will the silent treatments choke us

Will the violence around us provoke us

Will we ever truly know.

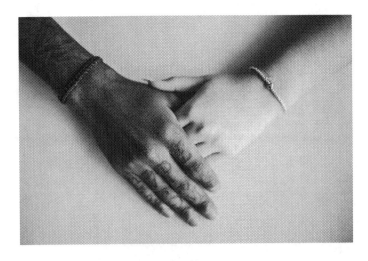

After Irina, I went without a girlfriend the entire seventh grade and by eighth grade I met Pamela. Now Pamela was something different. Pamela was a little mature for her age and that was mainly because she had to look after and care for her younger siblings. When Pamela and I met, I walked up to her and simply told her she was my girlfriend. I admit, it was a rather bold move on my part. But I figured if it didn't work, she would have at least gotten a good laugh out of it and would have thought I was funny. My older sisters have always told me that all girls like a guy that can make them laugh. Initially Pamela laughed at me but then got very comfortable with the idea as we continue to talk. Pamela and I would skip class together so we could find stairways to make out. I remember this one day we decided to skip class and meet under our favorite staircase during the last period of the day. Pamela always assumed I had more experience with girls then I actually had but I allowed her to believe it because it gave me some cool points and credibility. We met at our usual meeting spot and began to kiss. Kissing led to touching, and touching led to me sliding my finger in her panties.

Now understand this people…!

Before Pamela, that afternoon was the furthest I had ever reached with a girl. But remember she didn't know it so, I had to play cool as if I was use to it. Right there under the staircase, I took off her panties and I laid her down on the floor. I laid on top of her and unzipped my pants. I Pulled out my penis and slid inside of her. For the very first time, she was unknowingly taking my virginity. Many things were running through my mind in that moment but again, I played it very cool for her. The greatest feeling I had ever experienced in my whole entire life right there under the staircase. My very first sexual encounter happened at my junior high school. (It still blows my mind even now, many years later). In my head as we were "doing it", I was having the greatest party of all time. I was celebrating and jumping for joy but because she assumed I was experienced, I kept my cool.

The craziest thing happened as we were "doing it" (by the way, I keep using the quotation marks in celebration of that lucky little guy that was getting it in), the Principal walked out on the steps to have a conversation with one of the female teachers about where they were going to have dinner after school let out. At the time, I made nothing of it cause all I was thinking about was "holy shit, we are gonna get expelled from school". But now thinking back, it's more like "holy shit, they were having an affair" cause the principal was a married man. But I was not about to let him throw me off my game. So, I stuffed her panties into her mouth to keep her quiet and continued sliding in and out of her as I enjoying the greatest moment of my life. I'm not sure if it was the excitement of getting caught or just that it was so damn amazing but, I was beside myself. Lucky for me Pamela had not yet gotten her first minstrel and was not able to get pregnant. Nervously after it was all done I was ready to run over to all my friends and tell them all of what just happened. She must have read it in my eyes but she made me promise not to tell any of my boys and that promise I kept till this very day.

The undeniable truth for Pamela and I was that we had experienced sex, and we just wanted more of it. Pamela's mother worked nights at the hospital so one night after putting her little sister to sleep, she took a cab over to my place. My mother was also working nights as a home health aid so we had the entire night to ourselves on the couch. I remember that night when she came over, she had a black bodysuit on and some khaki skirt. Neither one of us could have waited to have that experience once again. Impatiently I wanted to jump on her from the time she walked in the apartment. So, sure enough we jumped on one another and never even took off her skirt. We just detached the bodysuit from in between her legs and there on the couch she sat on top of me. For the second time, I penetrated her and she felt even more heavenly than the first.

Sex truly does bond people together.

Once you have given someone your most valuable possession to someone, once you've had sex with someone, it's just a connection like no other. You and that person now become part of this cosmic universe and share a connection that could never be explained. I could tell that night by looking into her eyes that she love me. But I was just a boy and my understanding in that moment, my excitement was not at all of love but of the fact that I just had sex. I was happy to have a free apartment all to myself and to be able to have sex over and over and over again with my girlfriend. That right there is every young man's dream. Early that next morning, she took a cab back to her house so she could make it home before her mother returned from work. From that night Pamela was ready to completely commit to me but, I wasn't ready for any type of commitment. Needless to say she was way more mature then I was. In my fear of committing to a relationship, I faded away and made myself scarce. She tolerated my childish behavior but for so long and her frustrations grew stronger to the point she just stopped trying.

Pamela and I lost touch for a few years and doing that time, I moved in with my father as he and my mother came up with the plan of he and I building some kind of father and son relationship. At the time, my dad had a young 19 year old Jamaican girlfriend living with him. She was a very dark skinned girl with the most seductive set of eyes. Her name was Lotus and she was oh so beautiful but noticeably very hairy. Shaving was not that big of a deal in those days and in a weird way her hairy body was sexy (don't judge me people). I was supposed to be staying with my dad for a few months during the summer. His girlfriend was extremely welcoming from the day I got there. I remember she use to have me sit in between her legs as she played with my hair. By the second day she asked me if I was still a virgin and with the most macho tone I was able to muster, I replied "hale no "and every morning after that she would come lay with me in my bed almost as soon as my dad left the house for work. I would wonder every night if my dad had any clue his girlfriend was joining me in my bed. I guess that would be the proper train of thought when you knowingly continue to do something that you know to be wrong. The guilty conscience process I suppose. In her strong Jamaican accent she use to whisper in my ear "I'm going to make you a man". Every morning like clockwork for an entire summer she gave me oral to wake me up if I wasn't already awake and she would make me get on top of her. Thinking back, I now remember the very last time I saw Lotus was on a fishing trip that my dad took us on with his coworkers. She and I kept disappearing to make out on the side of the boat and she would slide her fingers inside her panties and put it in my mouth. That excitement didn't last very long that day as she became seasick and threw up all over the place. That afternoon after the fishing trip, I returned home to my mother without ever saying a proper goodbye.

A few months later after returning home, Pamela and I ran into each other on the street as she was getting Into a dollar van on Flatbush Ave. You are probably wondering what a dollar van is but you'd have to be from Brooklyn to understand the many forms of public transportation we have. From that afternoon we reconnected and it was as if we never missed a beat. I was in high school then and a bit more mature. I think on some level she noticed my maturity too but nonetheless wanted to see if my sex game had improved. She invited me over to her house 2 days later. Again it was at night while her mother was at work, she gave me specific instructions to go around behind the house and the back door would be left open. When I arrived, the back door was in fact unlocked but she was at the door wearing a white t-shirt and pink panties waiting for me. She took my hand and led me to a room where she stripped naked and laid there looking back at me with the most seductive look in her eyes and I just knew she was ready to be pleased. I think that night was probably one of the best experiences we ever shared together.

We were both entertaining different people at the same time so, naturally we lost touch once again.

Much like all young man in the history of mankind, we all get to a point where we simply feel to grown to take orders from our parents and as all Caribbean parents will tell you "2 grownups cannot stay undertake same roof". Once that time comes, the only option let is to move out and find your way in this life that you think you are ready for. I left my mother's home in Brooklyn and moved to a town which is located upstate New York about 45 minutes from the city. I moved in with my cousin D. Having moved in with my cousin, he took me all around town and introduced me to just about the whole town.

One of those people he introduced me to was Antoinette.

I don't even know where to begin in describing this woman

I can visualize her big bright smile this very moment as I write this. Her beautiful brown eyes and her video vixen like hips. Yes, that woman had a set of hips on her and to watch her walk was surely a thing of beauty. Antoinette and I believe it or not never had a sexual relationship or encounter. We kissed or should I say our lips touched on numerous occasions but it was never sexual with us. I remember one afternoon she and I were in her car and she was driving along the streets, I reached my hand across to caress her thigh and she turned to look over at me and completely taking her eyes off the road losing herself in the moment and drove into the vehicle ahead of us. We were so oblivious to the flow of traffic and that it was slowing down to a halt. With Antoinette and I, it was always about the magnetic connection that always drew us to one another. I don't even know how to put it into words really and it always did puzzle me but her energy captivated me from the day we met. Whenever we were together, we found satisfaction in cuddling, holding hands and looking into each other's eyes like a true Disney fairytale. We talked a lot and shared a lot about ourselves. Till this very day we are Instagram friends but these days our conversations are nonexistent. We keep up with each other's lives through posted images and likes. This thing called life…, there is never any true guarantees as to which direction it will take you but what an adventure it can be.

The first time I asked a woman to marry me:

Her name is Rachel and I say is because even though our relationship died years ago, she however is still very much alive. I met her through my cousin who actually went out on a date with her and quickly realized she was too

13

much of a good girl for him (in his own words) and decided she and I would be a perfect match. My cousin introduced us one afternoon after inviting her to his band rehearsal. She and I met and talked for the first time for at least six hours, so needless to say we were perfectly matched from the beginning. We plan to go out on a first date and for that first date I planned a picnic. From our first meet and the endless conversations, I gathered she was a hopeless romantic. There is nothing more challenging than planning a date for a woman who is totally infatuated with the notion of romance. I struggled back and forth with the picnic idea because I didn't want it to come off as a cheesy move. In the end I decided to go through with it as everything else would have taken the focus away from us talking and getting to know one another. I had everything ready and asked her to meet me in the backyard of a junior high school. (I know you are thinking right now "another junior high school"… but I swear it was purely coincidental). In a town in which after dark, it gets pretty quiet and the stars light up the entire sky. That night for our picnic, I forgot the picnic blanket but we made due and had a picnic on the hood of the car. At the time I drove a silver Mitsubishi Galant with a pretty serious sound system that my cousin installed. We ate, had some fruits and we had some wine. We shared stories of our past as we listened to her favorite artist Kenny G. We made each other laugh so hard that our cheeks begun to hurt. There that night under the stars and on our very first official date, we made love on the hood of the car. I knew for sure that night she was going to be my wife.

There is one thing I know for certain in this life and that is throughout the history of all my sexual encounters, I just knew right then and there once it ended if I ever wanted to see that woman again. Something about the transfer of energy in the air and the cloud in my head clearing up after an orgasm instantly would put me in a state of clarity and realism So for me to say in that moment she was going to be my wife means I was now in complete infatuation with her. We continued to see each other on a daily basis and a few months later she introduced me to her family. Rachel's family wasn't too fund of me being a construction worker and on top of that I was dark skinned. There is this thing in some African American households that turns them off completely when it comes to accepting a dark skinned male of their own race. Makes absolutely no sense at all but it happens so now I had that working against me and her entire family was light skinned. The other thing is that she was an instructor at the community college RCC. Much like all families, they wanted someone a bit more prestigious and I can't honestly fault her parents for wanting better for their child. Rachel cared nothing about their opinions for I had already won her heart. Rachel bought me my very first cell phone and when she gave it to me she said "here is my most selfish gift because I am doing it so I can reach you whenever I want. She and her sister Betty owned their own house in a part of town called Harvestraw. Rachel asked me to move in because she didn't want us to spend a minute apart aside from the hours we spent working. Rachel and I were not quite on the same page in the beginning emotionally.

She fell involve much quicker than I did but her love for me and the many ways she expressed it was my reason to fall involve with her. Such love rarely come around and before her I had never experienced that. She and I were never apart and my family hated her for that. She took up all my time and I never visited. Rachel talked me out of working construction and went to work for a temp agency in her attempt to convince her family that I was worthy of their acceptance. The temp agency sent me to work for the Yellow pages in taking add orders and even calling people offering special prices to advertise their businesses in what was then the white pages. Rachel's family never really accepted the relationship in spite of my change in what they called a respectable work space. I saw nothing wrong in a hard day of labor and at the end on the day I was always able to look back and physically see what I had accomplished that day. Her family always wanted her to marry someone of a higher status in life. My mother never cared for Rachel much either because she was about 7 years older than me. That experience with Rachel thought me to never under estimate the pressures of family's influence over a relationship.

At the time I believed her love for me was all that mattered and that they could never turn her against me as long as I kept her happy. But love has never proven to be enough. Like the song said "what's love got to do with it". For Rachel's birthday, I remember getting her favorite singer in the whole world to call her and sing happy birthday the morning of her birthday. I remember her shedding tears of joy for our love and promising that she would never ever let go and that she would rather die than to let us fall apart.

Rachel ended up meeting some guy through her family and I only found out because we went out one night and as we were walking in, the guy was there too and confronted her. That night we both walked away to never speak again till this very day. Little did I know but hat breakup was soon going to be my worst breakup in history. There I was 3 days after the confrontation, I woke up out of bed one morning to my entire left side being numb and completely limp. I called out to my sister who was staying with me at the time and she rushed me to the hospital. At the hospital the doctor ran a few tests and psychologist casein the room to ask me a couple questions to determine my state of mind. Before telling me that I suffered from Bell Palsy. Bell Palsy is a severe nerve damage caused by severe stress to the brain and the body. The severe amount of stress causes the left side of the brain to shut down and in reaction shuts down the mobility on the left side of the body. As you can imagine this was the most terrifying moment of my life. The many hours in the hospital, brought nothing but terrifying thoughts through my head of the horrible possibilities. I shed many tears that night unknowing what my condition would come out to be. The idea of being paralyzed for the rest of my life was too much to bare.

After hours of being poked and prodded by a multitude members of the Emergency room. The grueling hours slowing passed as I stared at the clock and suddenly the waiting was over and the doctor came back in the room. I was surely tired of waiting but was not at all ready to hear what the doctor was about to say. The doctor suggested physical therapy along with medication consistently in order for me to reverse the process and get back to normal.

The doctor advised me to stay away from anything or anyone that would put me in a stressful state because Bell Palsy is a condition that could always return.

The doctor also mentioned refraining from the relationship circumstances that may cause the condition to prolong. Therefore I found it to be in my best interest to at least try to live a stress free life. Life happens and by that I mean we all will go through some hard times at some point and the key is to learn about ourselves through those hardships. I knew if ever I was to commit to anything, I would see it through. I vowed to never again speak to or of Rachel. My focus was no longer on the love that was no longer in my life but on all the physical therapy sessions. My sessions were once a day but 3 times per week. In the house, I would repeat the same exercises up to 3 times a day. My sister assured that I took my medication on a regular basis as required. I regained mobility in my extremities within the six months of physical therapy prescribed. After Rachel I made the decision to move out of state that way I would be guaranteed to never accidentally run into her as it was the very last thing I wanted to happen.

After Rachel, I swore to myself that I would not allow anyone or any love or relationship to affect me to that extent ever again. Funny thing about love is that we can never really control it. Love can never really be tamed for it is unexpected, unpredictable, and unforgiven.

True love that is.

True love requires you to allow yourself the possibility of her pain, anger but every now and then you find the love that is worth every bit of that pain and suffering. But first you must have that willingness to leap with the understanding of no certainties.

In my plan to avoid all familiar territory, I made the move out to Hyattsville, Maryland. My oldest sister was living out there at the time and I moved in with her. While in Maryland I was able to obtain a position as an apprentice with the brotherhood union for carpenters. As an apprentice my first project was working on the stand on the White House lawn as well as the press box across the street from the White House in preparation for President Bush's inauguration upon winning his first term election. On that project, I also got the chance to work side by side with my sister's boyfriend Yolex and took a liking to him at that point. He was always a cool dude but I've always felt that he talked too damn much and like to post about his accomplishment a bit too much. However Yolex was about to earn his keep and make me proud as he suggested we drove out to Ocean city beach with a group of his friends.

Since moving to Maryland, I had never been out other than work because I just wasn't interested in meeting people and after all my view point was that I was only going to get disappointed through the ordeal anyhow.

But, my sister talked me into going and I did. The group all met up at a gas station nearby and I noticed a group of pretty woman in one of the cars but most of them were there with their mates. One of the girls caught my attention with her flirtatious smile and introduced herself as Mimi. It was the very first time I encountered her and didn't say a word until we were actually out walking along the sanded beach Still I hadn't said much to her other than exchanging phone numbers and talked about the weather. When we return back to Maryland we began communicating back-and-forth and she invited me out to a family cookout. Mimi was always insecure about her body, how she looked but for me it didn't bother me as my focus was getting to know her personality. She was a sweet girl very giving, very loyal and very dependable as described by her friends and family. Mimi is the kind of person that would go to the moon and back for a friend and someone that's willing to do so much for a friend led me to wonder just how far she would go for the one she loved. Mimi and I decided to move in together after only weeks of knowing each other. Living together initially was beautiful, it was our first time sharing a space and it was her first time ever living with a guy. It was truly something special. But as time passed I begin noticing certain behavior about Mimi that were just unsettling. Initially I would brush it off as nervousness of living up to the expectations of a live in boyfriend. More time passed and I would wake up in the middle of the night But Mimi would not be in the bed next to me. As I look throughout the house for her, she most often would be up standing by the front door or even out on the balcony just looking into space or crying for some unknown reason. I at first thought she was sleep walking but that thought progressed to a suspicion of bipolar disorder as she would snap out of it a be cuddly and cute. I found myself looking at her with that crazy look very often and wondering in my head is she was Coocoo for Cocoa Puffs. I felt she had some issues that she probably never intended to disclose to me. I often asked if she would ever consider seeking professional help or just someone to talk to where she wouldn't feel judged. I tried expressing to her that maybe there were things that she would need to get off her chest and didn't necessarily feel comfortable sharing them with me. But every single time she would deny, deny, deny and dismissed the idea. But to witness the same behavior repeating itself over and over got to me. Emotionally, we were spacing out but we both continued to act as if there was nothing going on.

One day while she was doing my hair (at the time I had braids by the way), I received a call from one of my sisters ex-boyfriend's sister (if that makes sense). Apparently she was asking about me and got a hold of my number to contact me. There I was sitting between Mimi's legs getting my hair braided and I get this unexpected phone call from an unknown number. I answered and it was a woman's voice on the other end excitedly asking me "what's up?" I excused myself to step outside so I can have a chat. My curiosity had peeked in that moment and wanted to know who this was. She introduced herself as Mimza. She reminded me of who she was and how I would have known her. (Her brother dated my sister at one point but we never really were in the same circle). She and I talked for a while and made plans for me to travel back to New York so we can meet each other in person once again. Only this time it would be a date. I didn't stop to think one bit "hey I'm still in a relationship with Mimi" or maybe even making Mimza aware of my current status. Instead I focused on how to make that plan happened and I did, I committed and there was no turning back. I made up an excuse for Mimi as to why I had to go to NY and got myself on one of the buses headed back to New York that following weekend.

My Sole focused was on my upcoming date with Mimza. It did not occur to the hurt that I had just put Mimi through because she knew something was up but she accepted my BS excuse. Like most assholes that go around breaking hearts, I made it all logical in my head so I could take all the guilt off my shoulders. Once I did that, I was again able to focus what was about to happen. Returning to New York felt really good that afternoon. There is something about that city that just makes me feel alive, the air feels different and even my mannerism changes. Plain and simple, there just isn't no place like NYC.

The first day back was beautiful, it was the date I traveled miles for. We met and had an awesome time but all we did was an ordinary dinner and a movie. What made it special was her spontaneous personality. The amount of effort went into her outfit was really sexy to me The moment I saw her, I remember biting down on my finger and thinking "God Damn". Girl had a crazy sense of fashion but with a taste of elegance. Her presence simply commanded your attention and she had it, I was gamed at that point. We shared a lot of laughs through the night and ended it with a kiss. The following day she came over to my friend's place where I was staying and that was the day she stole my heart. My buddy had to work so I was all alone in the apartment when she came over. We sat on the couch as I flipped through the channels but she had absolutely no interest in anything that was on. Her presence alone already had me turned on and by the look on her face, I could tell she was yearning for something more. I grabbed her hand and led her to the bed.

She allowed me to open that damn cookie jar and I ate, I ate, I ate like a fat kid in a candy shop!!!

The sex was effortless. It was as if we were one body, one soul totally and blissfully intertwined. Now looking at what we had at hand… Mimi and I were falling apart and there I was with whom I shared a lot of interest in the same things. We both had a love for fashion and shopped at the same places. Our sex drive was equally balanced and we both shared a love for music and dancing

(Especially the sounds we made love to).

We both had a thing for sex in public places.

I just want to take a moment here and acknowledge the fact that I now realize just how quickly I tend to rush into living arrangements with Women that I barely ever give myself the chance to know. Mimza Didn't like the idea of me commuting back-and-forth to Maryland so asked me to stay and move in with her and her mother. Without any hesitation nor warning I told Mimi it wasn't working out and I was moving back to New York. Very selfishly I might add as I packed my things and left. I was back in New York and I was living with a girl that I fell in love with overnight. After about a week, I decided to get back into construction for it was the easiest job to land and I have experience doing it. Mimza agreed to drive me to and from work until I was able to get my own car with the exception of days when she herself had to work and or had classes to attend. On those days, I would resort to public transportation which could take anywhere from 2 to 3 hours depending on traffic. After a long day of hard labor, the last thing anyone wants is a 2 to 3 hour commute on public transportation. That was the first time I looked back and wondered if the grass was really greener on the other side. Her mother for lack of a better word fell in love with me and loved me as her son in-law.

The very frustrating commute slowly became a routine and bothered me less but also made me appreciate so very much the days when she did take me to work and pick me up. Did I even mention the mornings when she would drive me to work, the amazing ways that she would jumpstart my day before dropping me off. In spite of what kind of night we had the day before, whenever we would get to the parking lot near my job; we used to have sex just about every morning. In the evenings when she would pick me up, we again would have sex in that very same spot. One day she picked me up and we had an argument so something stupid but somewhere in between her yelling at me, I kissed her and we did it on the trunk of the car. The spot where we used to park the car faced a main road call. It was a local street but had very few traffic lights so therefore commuters used it as if it was an open highway. There we were on the trunk of the car thrilled over the idea of having sex while cars along route would drive-by and catch glimpses of us. Sure enough they shouted at us but to know that we were seen became an even more of a turn on. We had sex in public places more often than I can remember because privacy was always an issue in the house. We shared the apartment with her mother, her grandmother and her cousin. At night we sometimes would wait till everyone fall asleep and sneak in the kitchen to have sex but even then it would have to be very quiet. After a while Mimza became frustrated of the whole living arrangement and wanted to get our own place. The frustration continued to grow and became a nuisance in a relationship. At one point, I packed up and went out to Florida to stay with my cousin to avoid the petty daily back and forth. A few days went by and she called demanding that I returned immediately. So I got on the next bus out Florida back to New York. After the very long 18 hour bus ride, she pick me up from the bus station and we got into another argument on the way back to the house. She stopped and pulled in an empty parking lot of a nursing home that was no longer in business. There she confronted me about encounters I might have had while in Florida and asked if in fact I cheated on her. Without any hesitation, I dismissed any allegations or any sense of insecurity that she might've had but she didn't believe. She was the type to get angry and get physical.

We were talking and as I was about to answer her question, she slapped, punched, and turned with her back against the car door to kick me as I was trying to grab hold of her hands. Soon as I got control of both hands, she bit me. She dug her teeth in my shoulder real good that day. I have never been nor do I think I will ever be the kind of guy that would put hands on a woman, but damn it she was pushing it that day.!

So, I grabbed her firmly and held her for about 5 minutes. She was squirming as she tried to break free from my grip but I whispered over and over in her ear "please clam down baby, please calm down". I didn't want to raise my voice because I knew it would only upset her even more. Her breathing started to slow down and I felt her softening up in my arms as I was holding her from behind. She slowly turned to look at me and I kissed her. A very slow, soft kiss that gradually became intense because we were both hurting from the distance and time apart. All the anger she had built up inside was from missing me and she faulted me for leaving. We continue to kiss as I stripped her clothes off. I had her completely naked in the backseat of the car on a steaming hot summer day. With the sun beaming over us and the car itself was steaming hot, we were both sweating. I turned her over with her hands and knees on the backseat of the car while I stood in the passenger side door way. I don't know if it was the heated argument before hand or just that I the taste of her sweet nectar but I was as as hard as a rock. I slid into her dripping wetness and gave it to her so hard, she begged for me to slow down as she screamed my name. She crawled to the other side of the backseat and pulled me into the car. In that hot steamy car she got on top of me as we sweat every ounce of fluid in our bodies. But she never stopped riding, she continued to kiss me, and bit me a couple more times until we both had an orgasm. If anyone of you have ever experienced this, you will understand when I say that orgasm locked my toes, the nerves in my back and shot out of me like a damn missile. Once we gathered ourselves back up and got dressed, we drove out to our favorite spot to eat. Mimza's biggest problem was that she grew up with her older brother who in every since of the word was a lady killer. Having seen his operation on a day-to-day and the way he toyed with girl's emotions had her in fear of me doing the same thing. Whenever she wasn't with or around me, she assumed I was out jeopardizing relationship. There's an old quote that my mother use to say "in life, people will project their own behavior onto you due to their guilty conscience".

In just a moment my reason for saying that will unveil itself

Mimza and I were home watching tv one night and she suddenly got a phone call which she exited the room to answer. A few minutes later she returned to tell me her home girl was stuck at work and she had to go pick her up. So, me being the person that I am and the fact that something just wasn't adding up. Calmly I told her to go do what she had to do, but I was going with. We got in the car drove out to Palisades Center Mall but the entire way she hadn't said a word which is very unlike her. During that very quiet drive, I began to think to myself how that whole situation wasn't adding up. My girl was not the kind of person that would get out of her bed in the middle of the night to go pick up a friend unless that friend was on life support. My girl was a very selfish individual but she was still my baby because I loved her selfish ass.

When you are in a relationship with someone, please pay attention to that person's attitude and behavior both when alone as well as out in the public eye. Now we pulled up to the mall entrance and she stop the car. I already get the gist of what's going on because I done played inspector gadget in my head but I was willing to play along till she came off it on her own.

She looked over to me and said "I have a confession".

Still playing along, I asked "what's up babe, is everything ok?

In the most "what had happened" (voice) she said "ok, I know I said my home girl but it's not a female. It's a guy friend that I've known from high school but I didn't want you to get mad". At that point we were already there and the guy was already walking towards the car. When the guy got to the front passenger door, he had that shocking look on his face because he wasn't expecting me. Awkwardly we drove her friend to his so-called family's house that he had to call along the way to get the address to.

I got home from work the next day and she wasn't home. She didn't come home till late in the evening and the entire time her mother would periodically ask me "where is your woman?".

When she finally arrived, she played it off as if nothing happened and as if it was normal for her to disappear for hours at a time. Never have I been one to go on shouting matches so calmly I asked where she had been. Walking around the room as she undressed and mumbled under her breath "Oh remember my friend from last night, I just went over to his house to braid his hair".

I looked to the sky and said a quick prayer cause I too had braids the entire damn time she and I dated and not once did that bitch ever braid my hair. She always complain that her fingers would hurt too much afterwards. So, for this motherfucker to look me in the eye and say she was braiding another dude's hair...!

I just didn't know how to react to that one so I decided the best thing for me to do was to pack my things and leave.

So I did. I packed and I left to my mother's house.

Question..

Why do we always go back home to mom when the shit hits the fan?

She didn't attempt to stop me, she didn't even offer to give me a ride to the bus station. I called a cab and took the bus down to the city, back to Brooklyn. That hour and a half bus ride to the city was my therapy session as I repeatedly punched the back of the chair ahead of me. What I probably should have done to her but glad I didn't and walked away instead.

On that bus ride I made up my mind that I never again would have gotten back with her. I made it to the city and now had to ride the 2 train back to Brooklyn which is about a 30 minutes ride from the street in the night. By the time I arrived at my mother's, she had already driven her car down to Brooklyn and was waiting for me in front of my mother's building. I guess she was gone for the whole dramatic affect but after what had happened, she had already lost me. She just hadn't realized it yet. I saw her car but I walked right passed it. She got out and followed me into the building demanded that I return back to town with her. I stopped in front of the elevator and looked her dead in the eye and told her

"If you wanted me, you never should have done what you did and you should have kept me from coming down to Brooklyn when you saw me packing".

I had to give myself a quick pep talk and asked myself "why would you go back after she disrespected the relationship and all that we shared". She continued to insist as I attempted to walk away, and that when she took a pen out of her pocketbook and stabbed me with it in my left arm. I continued to walk away and didn't even look back once. I went into my mother's apartment and locked the door. She walked over to the door knocked continuously but I never answered until she walked away. A few months went by without any communication and this annual event that usually happens In Florida call Kompa festival came up. My cousin and I along with a few friends flew out to Florida for the festival. We all went out to one of the annual cookouts that typically happens around the time of the festival. As I was walking through the crowd she and I bumped into each other.

We were both surprised just as we were both intrigued.

The DJ was playing one of our favorite songs so, I asked her to dance and she accepted. We danced to a couple songs and after few dances; we snuck out to the parking lot and into her rental car. Too much time had passed since I felt her lips on me, since I tasted her. The craving for one another came to life the moment our eyes met. We practically tore each other's clothes off in the backseat of that car. She straddled me while she whispered in my ear how much she missed me and asked if I missed her too. We held each other tightly for a very long time while still inside of her. We sat in the back of the car completely naked as we caught up on what's been going on since we were last together. We lost track of time to the point the entire party ended and we were still in the backseat of the car. We redressed and stood by the car pretended as if we were standing outside the whole time. Her brother along with a few other friends walked out. We never got back together after that night but we never fully lost touch.

To this day, we are very good Instagram friends…

MY FIRST WIFE

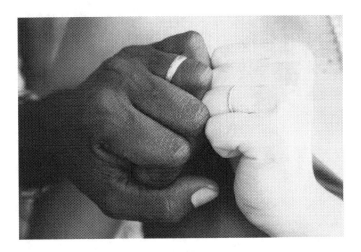

My first wife and I met in Brooklyn NY.

Myself and 3 other friends who till this very day share a love for the art of fashion got together and opened our own clothing store on an Avenue which is considered the heart of Brooklyn... There I was sitting at the counter one afternoon looking over some designs and planning for an upcoming fashion show we were Hosting at a University. She walked in to purchase some concert tickets from the guys next door to us but we shared the same entrance. I noticed her from the moment she walked in, pretty little young thing and that day she was wearing some skin tight khaki pants, brown waist line leather jacket and brown boots with a very skinny 4 inch hill. As she was about to walk back out, I asked her if she would like to look around a bit and that she might find something she liked. She agreed And as she browsed, I convinced her to try on a couple items. She was hesitant at first and told me flat out she wasn't going to buy anything simply because she tried it on. I truly wasn't trying to make a sale in that moment, I just wanted to keep her there long enough to talk to her some more. I had her try on a sweatshirt with the zipper that ran from the waist around the body and up to the neck. I knew it wasn't going to fit from the jump because she was very busty and the shirt was a small. She was having a bit difficulty With the zipper so, I offered my assistance. "Accidentally" I touched her breast while assisting but she didn't seem to mind too much. She was press for time because the concert tickets she had just purchased was to a concert that very same night. I offered her my information and she left me hers. I reached out to her that same afternoon to ask if she was attending the concert with anyone and she said yes, a few of her girlfriends. I gave her the heads up that I too Was going to that concert and perhaps she should save me a dance. We had a few good laugh about it and talked about each other's back grounds and family history. We met that night at the concert and sure enough she spent the entire night latched to my arm as if we had been a couple for years. The concert turned out awesome and In the end I walked her and her friends to their car and we went off in separate directions. She called me as soon as she got home that night and our conversations went on for hours, then days and turned into weeks. After a few weeks of conversations, we came to the conclusion that the concert wasn't a proper first date and we Made plans for one. For the first date, we went to see a movie on downtown Brooklyn. I couldn't tell you which movie we saw but we had a good time, We hopped On a dollar van back to her place and we talked some more at the door way. We said our goodbyes and I headed home. Back then texting wasn't really a thing so, we emailed each other pictures. We had a little game we played with the pictures and for each picture received, one had to be sent back as an exact match. Nothing too crazy just pictures of each other, getting to know each other better.

Nude pictures were as popular as they are today.

At the time my business partner was also seeing young lady named Kat. Kat lived about two blocks away from the boutique and wanted to have a little get together. So, I gave Nou the address and time to come meet us.

Little did I know the get together was only going to be the four of us. We got there my business partner and Kat went into their room leaving Nou and I in the living room all by ourselves. Minutes after their disappearance, I leaned over and began kissing on Nou's neck. She was liking it and was biting her lip so, I pulled off her shirt and touched on her breast. Before you know it, I had her completely naked on that couch. This was the first time I was seeing her nakedness, this was the first time my hands were exploring her skin, her curves so I was in no hurry. I wanted to enjoy every single minute. The entire time she was very nervous and I could tell this was not an easy process for her. To let her guard down, to open herself up to me and let's not forget we were in someone else's house. But she didn't fight it and she allowed me to touch her. She allowed me to take down her walls and she opened up herself to me. That night I noticed that sex with her was never going to be the kind I was used to. She was very guarded, she was very reserved. For a while I assumed she was preserving herself for marriage. Later I came to find that she had only been with 1 guy before me. We continue to date for a few more months after and I flew out to Florida to visit my sister who had an epileptic episode while she was cooking and burned her arms on the stove. While in Florida I went to a few parties with my sister's boyfriend and looking through the club, the girls, the dress codes and what they were doing to draw attention to themselves. It just wasn't for me, I was at a different stage of my life at that point. I drifted off in thoughts of the girl that I left home and the qualities, the characteristics I found in her. She was well educated, respectful, family oriented, caring, giving and a home body much like myself. So, while in Florida I had my sister's boyfriend take me to the mall and I purchased an engagement ring. I flew back to New York the next day and directly from the airport, I took a cab to her house. At the time I got there, it must've been about midnight. She came to the door after I knocked and as soon as she opened it. I dropped right down to a knee and asked her to marry me. Overjoyed, overwhelmed and in tears, she said yes.

She invited me and put on the ring. She quickly texted all her friends to let them know "he proposed". She than told her entire family, they were excited, they were happy and they welcomed me in the family. We wanted to wait to have a big wedding but about three months later she got pregnant and we had not yet planned the wedding. Her family didn't want her to have a child without first being married and to that they were very insistent. So, we went on to the justice of the peace in made it official. We began to look for an apartment so we could move in together. We found our first apartment a block away from her mother's house but the best part is that it was in the same building as my mother. We moved in and settling in came easier than we expected. She had a smooth pregnancy and the due date was upon us. The excitement of having our first child made everything else seem so minuscule. 10 hours in the hospital and then came the birth of my angel. We named her Eleana which in translation means the answer to my prayers. Once the baby arrived she moved in with her mom which was understandable with this being her first child, I knew she was going to rely on her support team which was her mom and grandma. The issue began when she was spending more time at her mother's then at our place. The days turned into months and before I knew it she was dropping by to visit for a few hours and headed back to her mother's leaving me yet again in the apartment by myself. Those couple of months now became a couple of years of me living along in my apartment while she and the baby were living with her mother. At this point the baby was no longer a baby and the story line changed from them being her support system to "how can I take the baby away from them when they have gotten so use to her being around". I don't think she factored in how this whole situation was impacting me. Needless to say there was no sex life or any kind of a relationship for that matter. We now were 2 friends that happened to be married. Initially it was hard to let go of that emotional connect we shared. Imagine if you can, we had just gotten married but never actual had the chance to live out that newlywed stage of the marriage. Once I was able to cope with the reality of what in my opinion was a failed marriage, I now had a new urge to explore the window of opportunity.

It was an opportunity to explore my many desires that were not being met at home. I've always had a very healthy sex drive and desires for the unconventional. I opened Pandora's Box and I completely lost control of it all. I was having countless encounters with random woman that I would meet at parties or even at work. I at the time worked as an EMT and the uniform was surely the babe magnet. It worked on just about everybody from nurses, doctors, people on the street and the most frequent ones were the family members of the patients I encountered. To make a long story short, our marriage ended before it even had a chance to start. We co-parented for years and every now and again we would talk and make broken promises to one another of becoming better partners. After 10 years of trying but at the same time living separate lives. Each and every time we "tried", I was either dating or entertaining other woman. In a few short conversations years down the line as we were filing for a divorce, the questions were answered. I then realized my role in why she chose to stay with her mother and she too understood my stresses of not having a wife at home when I needed it most. In those short conversations she disclosed to me that she was once molested by her mother's live in boyfriend. Even more traumatizing, the mother stayed with the guy after she spoke out on the abuse. Listening to the pain in her voice as she opened up to me, I now had an understand of why she was never really a sexual person nor ever place sex as a priority in our relationship. Therapy is not for everyone but in the same token we tend to shy away from it when we need it most. I hope one day she does try it out and it makes a difference in her life as well as future relationships. It's too late for us but never too late for her healing. Certainly didn't make it any easier on her with the constant confrontations of me cheating, she even found pictures of me with other woman in my car having sex. In those days I partied a lot and her friends constantly would send pictures of me with other women at bars. These things played a major role in her personality and behavior throughout the relationship. My actions made it even easier to maintain her distance, and security in staying with her family. I was only focusing the space and distance and lack of sexual contact, I stepped outside of my marriage, I cheated more times than I can remember. I will forever hold this woman in the highest regards, not only because she is my ex-wife, the mother of my 2 girls but for her strength. I admire her for the woman that she is and the kind of mother that I can count on her to be for my children.

COINCIDENCE

I think not..

Nothing happens by chance.

We find ourselves in places, amongst people solely based on the choices we make. I have been told that in all of my past relationships, I was never really in-love with the woman but instead in-love with the idea of falling in-love itself. I think back on this and I can remember ignoring a lot about that woman's individuality. I sure wanted to find in them what I personally was seeking. Seeking a connection so strong that the very thought of not finding it could have driven me mad. I have learned something about myself over these years. I have learned my ability to get others to fall in-love with me and I can do so very quickly. I am capable of this because in the beginnings, I dove in head first with no hesitation. I dove to the point of even loosing myself and drown completely into their personalities. At least the idea of them.

By them I mean whomever I was with at the time.

Whoever the subject of my desire was at said time.

It has never really been the woman at all but about love itself. My obsession with love. I absorbed the idea to the point of replacing their individuality and even their faces with the idea of love. Which explains why some of my exes weren't exactly cover girl material. In my dismissal of their physical attributes (looks) allowed me the ability to find in them all the things that love symbolized. Thinking on those encounters, I had been mismatched in every way imaginable. In some cases and in some ways, I was good to them. I have always wanted to be that one guy they could look back on years down the line and identify with what real love felt like. However long those circumstances were, they should perhaps have a recollection.

I am certainly infatuated with the notion of love.

Even when I knew the relationship wasn't going to last, I would still live in that moment with them to assure in them that our moment would one day be remembered as magical one. Right this minute you are probably thinking I have a sickness but it's my logic that magical moments equates love and love really is a series of illusions. Illusions that are believable to the naked eye and there for magical moments become love. Love is the master key that opens the heart. The master key that opens the heart has surely been proven to be in my possession by years of experience. The understanding of that possession has helped me to unlock many doors and some over and over again. My biggest struggle and really that struggle was within myself, but I could not then for the life of me understand why I was never able to keep those doors open on a consistent basis.

In every single relationship, I secretly had my own agenda and that agenda was to see just how much I was able get them to love me. I wanted to feel the love in my heart too but sadly I never did because it was never genuine. I was always able to feel the interest in the early beginnings but it also always died out as they lacked what it took to maintain my interest. It was not necessarily the worst agenda in the world to want a connection with another but the heartbreaks in the end made them very selfish and unfair.

I faulted myself.

I fault myself for not ever seeing those woman for who they were individually and seeing what they themselves wanted. Had I taken the time to see them individually instead of categorizing them all as one, had I given myself the time to heal from one heart break to the next perhaps I would not have broken so many others. Instead I always had the next person lined up by the time one relationship ended. It was always a continuation with me. I have fallen so far down that all I can see in my past "loves" are darkness.

I now fear that others can look into my eyes and see it too. I fear them looking into my eyes and see nothing but an empty space. Emptiness has consumed me and I have lost my master key. Not so sure I would even want to find that key ever again because what good is an open door that leads to nowhere. Had I not place the fault and flaws of one onto the other, I would have perhaps have been happier or at least free from the past. I am forever grateful for the lessons of my past but sadden those lessons were at the expense of others. I have decided that my past will no longer bear witness to my present.

MY MUSE

Around the same time I was going through this separation, I was also working and planning on opening a coffee shop downtown Brooklyn. My business partner and I had just secured a location and made a deposit. All my time and energy was devoted to that coffee shop. My partner and I worked on our budget and menu day and night. We finally had our ducks lined up after 8 months of research and the grueling construction project begun. We now had to turn an empty shell into what we envisioned. By shell I mean the 4 walls were all that came with the place. The ceiling, flooring, plumbing and electricity had to be completed out of our budget. We shopped around and found the best possible deals to get the job done. We designed the interior to be as unique as we possibly could. With everything going as planned, we went ahead and had our grand opening. The community took a liking to the cafe as soon as we opened and within the second week I met Marcy. She would drop in every morning for a tea and a plain bagel. One morning as she walked in, she noticed the help wanted sign on the window and suggested I hired her daughter for the position. A multitude of applicants inquired and I interviewed a hand full of them too but none of them had the personality of someone that I wanted to work with. Out of nowhere, unexpectedly a young woman with a very unique style, nerdy glasses, and short blond dreads walked in. Not only was she very fashionable but she had a freely, welcoming spirit. She completely captivated everyone's attention when she came in. She walked over to the counter and asked if she could work in the café (not if we were hiring) and without any hesitation I answered yes. She simply had me mesmerized in every which way. The way that she walked, her femininity, the beauty and purity in her smile. The innocence in her view of the world, her spirituality and love for all things and her willingness to embrace everyone. Every single day we spent in the café together felt like a date that lasted all day long. At the end of a 12 hour day, it actually saddened me to say goodbye. By the end of the first week, our sexual tension had reached its peak and after closing the café one evening, I called her down to my office. The office was in the basement of the cafe so I could hear her every step as she descended down the metal staircase. As she walked through the office door, I grabbed her by her waist and she leaned in for the kiss. I pinned her against the wall and we kissed. That kiss had been brewing from the first time she walked in the cafe. Such an electrifying aggressiveness overpowered us both in that moment, we were discovering one another. Every single touch, every single action and sound was magnified. Hearts pounding, nails gripping, passionately nibbling and biting on each other's shoulders. With her back against the wall, she slowly slid down to her knees and unzipped my pants. She exposed me but she took her time to look at it, she admired it with kisses and caressed it and then stroked it with both hands as she slowly inserted it in her mouth. She wrapped her lips firmly around it and marvelously sucked the soul out of my body. I swear in that moment I had an outer body experience. I felt my soul leaving my body and hovering over us in amazement. Every single one of my toes were curled as I grabbed hold of her dreads. As I was pulling on her dreads, she looked up at me with the spit dripping down the corners of her mouth. I grabbed her by her armpits and lifted her off the ground, turned her to face the wall as I took off her pants. Slightly bent over, I now was on my knees and boy was she dripping. I scooped it all up with my tongue.

She tasted different from anyone I had ever been with. I was licking and flicking her clit with my tongue but I just couldn't get enough of her wetness. In my head I was thinking just how bad I wanted to slide a straw inside her and slurp down on all that wetness. Her juices had me addicted and this was only my first taste. She pulled away and pushed me back onto the glass desk, she continued to suck on me until I exploded all in her mouth. She stood up, looked me in the eye as she swallowed every drop and kissed me. She then ran over to the bathroom to clean up. We finished locking up the store and I drove her home. As we sat in the car she looked over to me and said "sooo!!!!, That was interestingly different". We both laughed and grabbed each other's hand. I had that funny feeling come over me and I just never wanted to go of her. As I looked into her eyes, I just knew in that moment my life would never again be the same. She had a way about her that always challenged me, especially when she called me out on all my bullshit. She held absolutely no punches but never ever was she disrespectful in the ways that she challenged me. It really didn't matter what the issue was, she had a loving way of telling me off. She had a way of making me see her point of view and I loved her for it. By the second week she began staying nights at my apartment and she even had her own key. As crazy as this may sound, a 12 hour shift with this woman in the coffee shop felt like a walk in the park and each day I left the shop craving for more of her time.

We literally spent 2 years of working and living together and not once did I ever feel overwhelmed or the need for any space. We enjoyed the same things, so at the end of a long day, she always had ideas of things that we should or could do. She had a thing for bodies of water, she loved looking at the waves. We could go anywhere that had a body of water and just stare as far as our eye sight would allow us. For as long as we could stand it, our favorite place to hang out use to be the Brooklyn Promenade. The sight is just unbelievable, it overlooks the city skyline, vast bodies of water and right underneath the Brooklyn Bridge. One day she and I walk the bridge to and from Manhattan and ever since I have come to love that damn bridge. All along the bridge were locks with lover's names and even along the iron railings were names inscribed with the date visited. Love quotes written to inspire other wondering hearts and souls.

CONFESSION

A wise woman once told me in order to truly allow anyone to love me, I first have to be

Allow myself to be vulnerable and transparent with all my deepest darkest secrets.

I very often find myself wondering why my mind works the way that it does and why

I make certain decisions. I would really hate to end up alone and a sad old man like my father.

Nonetheless, I can't seem to change my cheating habits. The very first thing that comes to mind

When I meet or see a beautiful woman, is how good it would feel to fuck her. Sex tends to

Occupy my mind 24/7. I've tried praying so that I can change my ways but that does nothing.

Some say my prayers weren't sincere enough. It's almost as if I have an emotional disconnect

Switch and all that I see or care for is sex. Once that aspect is conquered, so is the interest in person.

This absolutely angers people because in the beginning, I can be very convincing.

The urgency to get away as if the world was ending comes over we.

I hardly ever find anyone that can maintain my interest after the sex is over.

This shit drives me crazy to the point that I even ask myself "What the Fuck"

I honestly love "Love".

I dream of it, I look for it, I wish for it but then maybe my idea of love is not realistic.

Maybe I have watched one too many movies.

The funny thing is that I found at least one good trait in every woman that I have ever slept with.

So if added together they would all have the makeup of my dream girl.

My Dream girl…

Is there such a thing?

Is it realistic to hold out for an imaginary thing that have yet to surface.

Some say that idea is an excuse to hide behind so I can continue to live the way I do.

But hey, we are all allowed to believe in what so ever we want & I have chosen to

Believe in a true and certainly obtainable love.

The Brooklyn Bridge holds a significant space in my heart. I must have walked that bridge a thousand times since. It is just my place of peace. My place to think and release.

It is the place Dia and I promised one another that we would always visit if ever we were ever broken up and in search of one another. Ironically it was the place that we agreed to meet on that New Year's Eve after our break up.

TO HOLD

I just want to hold you like a prayer that god himself handed me.

To get my arms around you and never again let go.

You give me that urge to be a better man, a superman.

If need be, I will run across the highest mountains and swim the deepest seas.

Where ever you are is where I need be.

For as long as I can remember my love,

You have always been all that I ever wanted and was seeking out.

There is a known saying that misery loves company which has been surely proven to be true

Every single time other have said or at least tried to tell me not to give my all into our union.

Some tried to remind me of "all the fish in the sea"

Some have asked "how are to be sure that she is the one"

I for the most part don't even try to entertain the ignorance of

Others but every now and again one just can't resist.

So I have told a few that life comes with absolutely no guarantees and especially

In matters of the heart. It is simply a leap that every single one of us will at some point have to take.

Unless we give our all, we will never truly know what

Could have been. . .

Let me take you back in time for our breakup.

Dia's mother and I became very good friends and in fact her mother use to advise me on business decisions regarding the café. Her mother was well established in the community. She was the principal of a junior high school, she owned a few rental properties along with the house she lived in and was interested in partnering up to open a bar. Somewhere along the lines of our friendship, her interest in me turned romantic. (A moment of honesty, I too found her attractive) Our compatibility was as unique as mine to her daughter. She was a married woman and I was in love with her daughter so by definition, that should have been tagged no man's land and never to be touched. She and I hung-out often to discuss business and for the most part my business partner was also present. The majority of those meetings were to discuss strategy and planning for the bar. One night she decided to come over my place because didn't feel like going home. Knowing what was on her mind and she was after, I immediately called my business partner who knew them both very well. When I explained the situation to her, she advised me to go right ahead and "take one for the team".

The one day that I wish I could take back, the one enormous mistake that I wish I go back in time and change was ever crossing that line and having sex with her mother. Now to play the devil's advocate for just a second, her mother did promise me that it would remain between us that no one would ever find out. Not using it as an excuse but damn it what ever happened to keeping your word these days (lol).

44

Does anyone honor the code of silence anymore?

The day Dia found out remains as fresh in my memory bank as the day I met her. Dia, her mother and my business partner all gathered at the café and called me in for a meeting. It was my day off and around the time of closing for the café. I had known my business partner for about 13 years so, I knew that tone she had on the phone was not a happy one. Now, I don't know why exactly but anytime I am summoned to any kind of meeting; I immediately get that uneasy feeling in my stomach. My mind began to wonder endlessly of the possibilities. I walked into the café and noticed them all sitting at the table near the back of the café. Every single one of them looked towards me with an angry look on their faces. My poker face turned intense immediately, because I already knew my wrong doing. No amount of "I'm sorry" was going to fix this one. The mother knew the fault that she played in breaking her daughter's heart but pretended as if she had absolutely no idea her daughter and I were seriously together. My business partner who told me to "take one for the team" looked me in the eye and with a very straight face asked "how could you ever be so disgusting and do something like this?" Finally, the look on Dia's face. She didn't say a word but the tears were constantly running down her face. She didn't even have to say it but the look she had screamed "how could you". The betrayal of the love that we shared, I became overwhelmed with emotions and walked out. Her mother shouting after me (you are an asshole), my business partner shouting my name asking me to come back and talk things out. But Dia followed after me and even though she was filled with anger and confusion, she still caught her breath to softly whisper "I love you". I reached out and grabbed her hand and pulled her in, I hugged her, I held her in my arms firmly for as long as I could. I knew in my heart it was going to be the very last time.

Forgiving my transgressions would require a lot out of a person and I myself could never have forgiven such betrayal. The entire time I held her in my arms, her tears continued to fall. I reached to the back of my head and ripped out a string of my locks and handed it to her for safekeeping. The back of my head began to bleed but at the moment it really didn't concern me much. To my surprise, she took off her gold chain and handed it to me as her remembrance. We both walked in opposite directions constantly looking back at one another. With every single step we took apart, the pain increased and the harder it was to breath. The next few days were even worst to deal with because I now had to face myself and own my actions. The days after, I physically showed up to the cafe but mentally I had checked out. Emotionally I was a wreck with no one to blame but myself. I wasn't focused at all on the business, wasn't aware of the finances nor the overhead to run the day to day operations. Business was diminishing; foot traffic became scarce as the competition grew. The competitions increased by the 2 new businesses providing the same services but were already established brands. Regular customers became nonexistent and wouldn't even look in as they walked pass the café. (The place they once called home and a gift to the community).

The weight of my wrongs weighed heavily on my mind for weeks on out. I even stopped going to the café and left my business partner to handle things. The hardest thing at times is to be honest with oneself because the reality of our wrongs are often too real and too hard for us to comprehend. I had reached my moment of honesty and lord knows it was not easy to bare. I even stayed home for a few months as I processed through my state of depression. I eventually mustered up the energy to begin work out again which over time progressed to taking late nigh runs around the neighborhood. By the 5th month, I accepted a job working as an account manager for a retail company. The daily interactions with account holders kept my mind busy and occupied throughout the day.

Those daily interactions were great but as nightfall came around, my nights would become dreadful. The worst thing in life is having to live with yourself after you knowingly screwed someone else over that in no way deserved it. When you knowingly betrayed the trust of a loved one. Dia's innocence hunted me and for an entire year I worried if ever I would be able to make things right and how much harder karma was going to hit me when it comes back around.

YOU ARE

You are my air

You are my everything

I now feel soooo… lost

I can't think straight

I can't go a single day without wondering where you are

Or how you are

What you must be going through

I feel as if my heart is bleeding out with every thought

I have this excruciating pain rushing all throughout my body

You were my best friend but now you treat me as an enemy

Praising your name to anyone willing to listen

Shouting just how fast I would jump at the chance to prove this love

My heart will never be healed without you

Love will forever remain a mystery till you and I are back as one

A slow dreadful path has now become my life

One thing that is certain in life, Karma always comes back around and it is not known to ever play fare

I would often find myself in the very same places she and I frequented in hopes of running into her. One day a mutual friend told me she was working at Bloomingdales. So needless to even say, on my next day off I visited Bloomies. I walked the entire floor browsing around anticipating seeing her for the first time in a year. Unfortunately, it never happened. Out of nowhere the next week, a miracle happened. She texted me and agreed to meet after she got out of work at a nearby bar. I went through that entire day with my heart literally pounding out of my chest. Even my clients throughout the day saw the excitement in my presence. Some even asked what the good news was about and proudly I replied each and every time

"my love has finally come home".

Awake

I wake up every morning and write down the many ways you have visited me in my dreams.

I write down these love notes hoping to one day make this dream come true.

To one day wake you up one morning covered in these little notes.

I will never fault you for having left

But I will forever regret the many moments we missed out on while we were apart.

Many things have happened and you were always my first call to share my joy with.

As of late, it has been somewhat bittersweet, I would give anything right this minute to hear your voice

In some ways, I wish the accomplishments never took place since I don't have you here to celebrate them with.

I then realize that the growth is not so bad because when you do return, it will be that much better to receive you.

That much more readily available to love you as you have always deserved.

I jumped on the train headed uptown after work. I walked over to the bar. I went inside and ordered a pitcher of beer and 2 shots of Jameson. After a couple glasses of beer, Dia walked in and I waved her over. Awkwardly, we did the "hey what's up "but after a few glasses and a few more shots, we were wrapped up and kissing each other's faces off. I even slipped my hand in her pants and dipped my finger in her sweet nectar and licked it off. I sure missed the taste of her. We laughed through the night as we caught up on all that has happened since we parted. We were having so much fun catching up, we didn't even realize the bar was closing or that it was 3am. We got on the train and rode back down to Brooklyn and during the train ride, Dia came up with the idea that we should meet on the Brooklyn Bridge on New Year's Eve if we decide to get back together. So, I was all in without a doubt. We got her stop and I remained on the train for a few more stops. From that day on, I marked and counted each passing day to New Year's Eve. The day finally came and had the most awesome day at work because once again "my love was coming back home". After work I stopped by the flower shop and picked up a dozen white long-stemmed roses. I picked me up a hot chocolate because it was freezing out that night and to be out on that bridge was going to be even colder. I walked to the middle of the bridge where we made out mark and waited. Quite some time passed but I waited and waited and waited some more. Something triggered me to log onto Instagram and there she was posting videos and pictures with her friends having, having a blast while I was freezing my butt off on the Bridge.

I walked back to the Brooklyn side of the bride and while walking, I looked over on the iron railing of the bridge and saw "timing is everything". I tried to process the words as I walked back across the bridge and suddenly it hit me. That night on the train, she said "if we decided to get back together "but I took it upon myself to believe we were meeting. I don't regret showing up even though I was there alone because had she gone and I didn't, it just would've been a good thing at all. I couldn't allow myself anymore chances to hurt that woman. After all the trauma, heartache and pain that I had put her through, that night was a disappointment that I was gladly willing to accept. I made a conscious choice to admire her from a far and I surely have enjoyed watching her blossom into who she has become.

MY CRY

I was once walking in the lime light

In a city so field with light that the stars never once shined

City of lights some uttered silently

A city created for the wondering souls

A city for the ever so creative enchantress

From the moment I noticed her.. I was suddenly changed

I was rearranged

Some would even say it was my born again.

After which I was no longer able to walk nor talk the talk of the life before

Those days of blindly reaching out

Blindly touching

Blindly dipping into bitterness but called it honey

It no longer measured up to the standard that I now held myself to

I now felt, touched and tasted purity

Acirfa Valentine

She freed my soul

All my burdens had simply been lifted

She took away my heaviness

I now had a better understanding

I knew who and where I wanted to be

Where I belonged

All because...

All because I cried

All because I surrendered to what was in my heart.

LIFE IS ENTIRELY TOO SHORT TO BE ANYTHING BUT HAPPY.....

I have been miserable and still am

As I lay here listening to songs that only remind me of you

Or make me want you even more.

Consciously, I do these things because it's the only way to keep you close.

But what I realize is that, when you truly are In-Love with someone

Nothing holds you back so with that I say the following...

The only thing left for you to say is whether or not your happiness includes us..

One can only play the fence but for so long and then like it or not,

We all get to the point where we must make a choice....

But know this, I am in-Love with you.

I am fully aware of who you are and see all the potential in who you can become.

As I told you before baby,

I wouldn't change a damn thing because "I love my Baby.

I need neither reasons, nor excuses but only to know if we are or if we are not.

The beautiful thing about love is that you never have to seek it out, it will find you some way somehow.

Which is the reason that I will always thank God for the few times that I was in the presence of Love,

It always came naturally. Nowadays I hear all the talks about how love doesn't exist anymore

But every time I see your smile, I know just how full of shit they are..

Eventually all things fall into place. Until then, laugh at the confusion, live for the moments,

And know everything happens for a reason.

From a distance

I see you over in a distant place,

Living,

Loving,

Laughing

And to that I am thankful

But still I am here stuck in this place called love.

In this place I wish to remain for it is my happiness.

I am striving to be more than I have ever been.

I wish to reach heights I have never dreamed of reaching before you.

After you, I could never go back to being blind and careless.

How I long for that day when you will once again see me

Acirfa Valentine

Hold me in your arms, your tenderness.

To wrap me in your forever,

Caress me with all of your seduction and keep me

Into the tight folds of your soul.

We were made to love baby,

I was made for you as you were made for me.

Together is where we belong

MY MORNING BLUES

Where has my smile gone?

You walked away and my smile disappeared along with you.

I would be smiling if I wasn't so desperate

I would even be patient if every second of the day didn't feel

As if you were getting further away.

From where I stand my choices are very simple,

I can never give up.

I must win back your heart.

All that I do is so that you can notice me

But nothing I do seem to grab your attention

I see you smiling but I keep missing the joke,

Again and again I wonder how she can find happiness

Without me..

Maybe it is easier from where you stand.

Acirfa Valentine

I did this..

I fucked up.

So, go right on ahead..

I probably would too if I were you.

After all that I have put you through,

I don't at all mind being your clown.

I just hope..

One day I too will laugh.

One day..

Time and space will no longer keep us apart.

But for now

I will be the clown.

My dear love..

Your laugh keeps me from crying.

So, continue to enjoy the laugh.

LOST

I spent the entire day in the city today.

I must have visited all the places that you and I have ever been to,

Because believe it or not these places still bring me comfort.

Comfort from knowing that we once were there together.

I feel so dazed and confused at times.

Here I am trying to maintain and this place where you have left me.

I even made myself into somewhat of a stalker of your shadows,

As I walked the isles of Bloomingdales envisioning your smile.

Without a plan or even expectations but, the thought of us seeing each other.

The thought of nature taking its course.

Listening to my Ipod on the way home, a song came on that I didn't even know was there.

The song is "down the line" ((written and sung by John Newman).

That song made me feel so much better because it made so much sense

It was like a sign from the unknown and I just chose to respect it.

On that day, I chose that leap of faith.

Faith in things working themselves out in the end.

Things tend to work themselves out when the time is right with the universe.

As the song said "right one just at the wrong time"

So, until destiny deems it to be the right time for us.

I will miss you.

The most beautiful thing about loving you is that I see you in just about Every

single thing that I do.

LOVING HER

I know I am her lover even without loving her.

I am alone but never have I felt lonely.

Comfortably, I can say I am deeply in-love with her.

I have decided to belong only to myself if she cannot be at my side.

I will love me as I know she would.

I will respect me as I know I would respect her.

I will no longer doubt her love,

I will no longer worry about where or who she may be with.

I definitely will no longer worry about who is loving her

Because I know at the end of the day.... she belongs with me.

When will our time be right.

When will she come back to me

The woman that I fell in-love with,

The woman that I will spend the rest of my life with

That very same woman who I wish for every night.

The one I kiss good night regardless of where she may be

Because she is always in my heart.

Soul mates have a funny way of finding their way home.

BUS RIDE

Needless to say I was thinking about you,

Because by now you should know that you are always on my mind.

So, there I was on the B6 riding home from my therapy session (physical therapy that is).

Not the other kind because I haven't fallen that far off the cliff as yet.

Well, maybe I have but people have not yet begun to notice or they would have me committed (LOL).

Going back to the bus ride...out of nowhere, it dawned on me that you may never come back.

Somehow all that we were will just be another thing of the past and you will never look back.

I kind of got lost in the thought process and missed my stop completely.

I finally got off the bus and walked the whole way back to the house.

Suddenly, I was overwhelmed with sadness.

Angry and confused, I shouted in the middle of the street "how could you just get over us that easily?"

"How could you get to the point of giving up?"

Acirfa Valentine

I remember us having that conversation on the bridge and you asked me

"If two people love one another as much as we do, when do you get to the point of giving up?"

"When do you say enough is enough?"

We both agreed that it would never come to that.

Neither one of us would ever truly find any peace,

nor any kind of happiness because we are each other's happiness.

Could it be possible that she is my true love, my once-in-a-lifetime but I am not hers?

I have always believed that soulmates came in pairs, so how could she not be mine?

How could she give her heart to another?

I still can't make any sense of it all because in my heart and soul I believe we were made for each other.

Someway somehow you will find your way back to me.

Every night I pray that you will wake up, wherever you may be

And realize that we can no longer be apart.

I picture you call me to pick up your things.

It is a damn dream, but it's my dream.

You are my dream

HAPPY VALENTINES

Happy Valentine's Day to the love of my life..

So much I wanted to spend this day with you,

Whether we were happy or mad at one another.

Just to be in each other's presence.

In this love that I have for you, I am content.

I never loved you out of convenience nor to simply please you

But because it was my heat's joy & desire.

For as long as this joy is in my heart, I will always love you.

The person I know, the one I cannot live without has moved on.

Publicly or in a quite private space, Valentines will never again mean the same.

Never again will I love anyone to pieces.

Still, I say I am not walking away,

You are my one and only.

I promise you baby I am worthy.

Acirfa Valentine

If only you could give us another chance,

You would see the change in me.

I long for you to see me,

Not just physically but to really see me for who I have become.

The person that I have become is because you inspired me.

The respect that I now have not just for you but for myself,

I learned through our struggle.

You will always be my one & only,

In this life or the next

AS WE RISE

Your words in my tongue

Your speech from my lung

Your songs that I sung

Your instruments that I strung

As we rise

The beat of your heart

In the well of my chest

The inhale of my breath

In the rise of your breast

The high of your soul

In the spirit of my best

As we rise

Acirfa Valentine

Your tears in my eyes

Your fears in my sighs

Your color in my dyes

Your blue In My skies

EMOTION

A demonstration from my imagination

In a form of an illusion

But it would be too much to conceal

The things I feel

They seem so real

So many times I feel

I could kill

At Will

But I do my best to remain still

As if I'm made of steal

I try and I try to ignore those feelings

Searching for a way to Heal

DISTANT

A distant thought of what once was,

What we once thought would last forever.

Some would call it foolish

Some said it was wishful thinking

But to know a love like yours,

How could I not dream of more?

How could I ever be content with just being ordinary?

No....

I want to dream

I want to be rudely awakened

I want to reach out

& touch the stars

Please look up..

See the stars..?

Reach out..

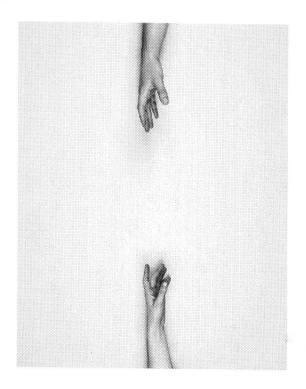

Guess I'll see you around.

I was on the force for 6 months the first time I saw her.

It was a sunny afternoon and at the time I was assigned to the foot beat division. Though it's called foot beat, we still had the option of either walking, riding a bike or a Segway. That afternoon, I was on a Segway. She responded as a backup unit on a call for a demented person and I just couldn't help but to stare. She simply had a presence that commends. Was not sure is she was unaware of her natural beauty or was just playing it cool. We never actually spoke but she noticed me just as I noticed her. Months passed by before I ever saw her again but when I did, we instantly clicked. The second time I saw her, I had just been reassigned from foot beat to the patrol division. On that day I found out she and I were going to work the same area but on different shifts. She was assigned from 7am to 3pm and I worked the same beat from 3pm to 11pm. I always came in as she would be on her way out the door, initially she would pass me right on by but over time, she occasionally would take the time to let me know what went on throughout the day and which perpetrators to look out for. Slowly we developed a really good working relationship before I ever even hinted any interest in her. I looked forward to the daily roll call because it assured me a moment alone with her. A few more months passed and my admiration of her grew stronger for her work ethics. I admired the kind of an officer she was. We even joked about competing over the number of arrests made. Through those few months of getting to know each other's work performance, we began to ride together as she would stay over after her shift for overtime. The winter months had come to pass and for that summer her 2 daughters ages 7 and 9 were gone for summer vacation.

She now had a lot more free time and she spent it with me working overtime. The more time together, the more I became even more fund of her. One day, while riding around the city in the patrol car and having yet another day at her side. I disclosed my enormous crush on her, she was not at all taken back and in fact she was relieved. It just so happens that she too was interested in me but as all woman tend to do, she pretended as if it was not at all a big deal. We continued to work and ride together for days on out and continuously discussed the possibilities of any relationship outside of working together. In the entertainment of those possibilities, we shared stories of passed disappointments along with future relationship goals. She filled me in with all her frustrations in the dating game. A game it really is for people have lost complete track of the point but turn it into plots of schemes. We were very open and honest with one another about what we wanted and would Not at all under Any circumstances put up with any longer because we now had an understanding of why things had not worked out in the past. It was almost creepy in a way. We were too much alike, we wanted the exact same things and she truly was one of a kind. In those summer months, she gave me a reason to believe it was finally safe to openly and fearlessly open my heart. I in return made her a promise that she would never again Shed another tear because I was ready to protect her heart as if it was a gift God himself handed me.. She was like a dream come true and mind you we had not yet been out on a date. Before our first date, she had already given me the confidence to face my fears in relationships. We agreed to go on a breakfast date on the condition that if it went well, we would go an actual outing for a formal date.

Part of me was a bit nervous but the rest of me was ecstatically ready to finally begin this journey. Relocating to Georgia was a sudden and bold move that took me away from family, friends and anything remotely familiar. Even though I had been in Georgia an entire year before Meeting her, I hadn't done much aside from hanging with my academy mates. The morning of the breakfast date, I really had nothing prepared as I barely knew my way around other than the area I patrol along with getting to and from work. She and I agreed to meet at a mutual place for our first date. The moment we met at our designated place, I just knew she was going to change my life. The energy we shared felt extremely comfortable as if we were already in a relationship. We joked about the very first time I met her and how she felt about the Blade haircut I had. Back then I use to cut my own hair and for some reason, I thought it was working. She laughed so beautifully, In fact; the sound of her laughter was very unique. Funny enough, she felt the same about the way I laugh as well. So, I didn't mind her roast sessions whenever she would ride alongside me. She certainly kept me on my toes on those day because she would make so many jokes about me or the people we encountered at work. I had to be quick with the comebacks so she wouldn't have the upper hand.

She grilled / interrogated me for hours in the car about the places I've been to since moving to Georgia and whether I visited those places with friends or on dates with potential lovers. She then finally suggested a place that I had never before eaten at and I was a bit apprehensive as I have been known to be somewhat of a picky eater. However, I was so happy to be out with her in that moment; I would have tried just about anything. The place was very cool and different and the food was amazing as she promised. We had very comfortable conversations about who we were and how we ended up to the point of being out together on a date. We were mentally seduced by one another and she got up out of her chair and leaned over to whisper in my ear "meet me in the bathroom". There was no time for hesitation, I got up and briskly walked her footsteps but as I approached the restroom door; something came over me. I suddenly became very aware of myself and my routines but I knew I wanted much more than sex out of her and I wanted more out of the connection that we shared. I already knew what would have happened if I walked into that restroom. So, instead I waited in front of the door for her and as she walked out with a humongous she too was glad I didn't go in. She herself said "I was So horny, if you came in you would have gotten it". Fact of life is that sex tends to change things and I was in no hurry to sleep with her as I was enjoying the process of getting to understand the kind of woman she was. When she came out the restroom, I explained to her that my interest in her was deeper than the needs of the flesh.

I wanted her to know that when the time came for us to have sex, what we would come to share would be something real and everlasting. Sex at time is just that "sex" but, sex with a person that you love and admire is magically inspiring. I covered the check as we walked out to the car and just being herself, the ever so playful, young at heart, she made me feel as if I had just found "my one". We stood there next to the car and held each other so firmly and without any music we danced right there on the curb. After my dance, I opened her door and after she sat down, she looked up at me and smiled (with that my heart melted). I drove her back to her car at which point we agreed to go on a formal date. I had to come correct for the formal date, after all it was going to mark the official beginning of our journey together. I did my research and found the perfect event online days later and purchased the tickets.

So came the very first official date.

It was a Saturday evening and we both worked that day. The excitement of this event being our first official date, means I still had to make a lasting impression. We agreed ahead of what time I would be picking her up at her mother's house. I must have changed clothes at least 5 times and left a pile of clothes on my bed by the time I was satisfied with the outfit and walked out the house. My pounding and overly excited heart would not allow me to be late. I nervously drove out to her mother's house and I pulled up to the driveway, impatiently await to see her walk out. I saw her every day at work in Uniform but other than that breakfast date, I had never seen her all dressed up and dolled up. For the first time, standing there awaiting her at the front door and (for lack of a better word) I was blown away. My heart literally stopped and my jar dropped. She wore a stunning black dress with a lace front on her cleavage with her back exposed. The dress complemented her curves perfectly and she accessorized the dress with a burgundy open toe strap hills. She is naturally beautiful and she doesn't wear makeup on a regular basis. I had never before seen her look so amazing and I just stood there for a few seconds to take it all in as she smiled back at me. I ran to the door and took her hand to help her down the steps. I stepped back as she walked to the car and enjoyed watching her walk in those hills. Absolutely loved the way that dress complemented her complexion. I opened her door and she sat in the car, I quickly did the sign of the cross and thanked God for blessing me with the opportunity as I walked around to the driver side. As much as we hate to admit it, all first dates are designed to evaluate one another and to see if we can live up to the initial expectations or pass the Dating tests of girlfriend or wife like qualities.

She passed the very first test as she reached over the driver seat and opened my door.

(That small gesture led me to believe early on that she was thoughtful, courteous, and that she was appreciative of me opening her door)

We drove out to the event and once we arrived I assisted her out the car so I could be her very own paparazzi and she deserved every bit of it too. I must have taken a million pictures of her that evening, she looked so beautiful, I just couldn't help it. We then made our way into the event and from the time we entered, we were the talk of the night. We were complemented throughout the night on how well we complimented one another, we were the youngest couple in attendance. My amazement, my complete infatuation of her was noticeably obvious as I found it impossible to take my eyes off her. She noticed it as well as she looked at me and asked "You really like me huh?". Enjoying a verity of wine and learning the art of testing qualities of wine, we gazed into each other's eyes as we were holding hands and I taking in the sight of her beautiful smile. The chemistry was perfectly intact, I didn't even have to try to make her laugh. After a verity of wine and finger foods, we went onto the dance floor.

The night simply could not have been any better.

The DJ mixed throwback R&B music and we both loved and sang along to every song. This is how I knew she was a keeper, she leaned in and whispered in my ear "my crotch is dripping wet with sweat". So, like the gentleman that I am. I walked over to the bar, grabbed a handful of napkins and walked back to her. I dropped to my knees and wiped between her legs gently and we continued dancing the night away. After a few more drinks and some more dancing, we both felt like we had enough of the crowd and decided to head out. We walked back to the car as I complemented her on how beautiful she looked and also on how firm her butt looked in that very fitted black dress. She turned and pointed to her butt and said "Kiss it". Now, don't quote me but I do believe the good book said something about "thy shall not temp the", so I did. I actually pulled up her dress so I could kiss her butt cheeks directly. She asked me to do it again in the car where people could not see her. I opened her door, sat her down and leaned the chair all the way back. I got in behind her stooping on my knees and I lifted her butt off the chair, pulled her panties to the side. Heavily breathing, she looked down at me and asked "what are you doing"?. I replied "I'm claiming my pussy". I tasted her sweet juices for the first time and I loved it. I even licked her butt hole. I continued to eat her out as she continued to get even wetter and she climaxed. I sucked and swallowed every drop of her juices. I then unbuckled my pants and and slid inside her.

For the first time, right there in that parking lot, she gave me her most valuable possession (The Pusssy) but the intimacy was cut short. We stopped so we could relocate to another location with less foot traffic. We both knew in that moment we were hooked. That moment was the very beginning of us falling in-love. We dress back up as she feared being seen. I started to drive back to her mother's house but along the way we both wanted more. I reached over and rubbed on her clit and she asked me to pull over. We were on the far left lane of I20, but that look in her eyes commended every nerve in my body. I moved all the way over to the shoulder on the right side of the highway. Quickly threw the car in park and right there on the side of the road, I lifted her over the middle counsel and bent her over between the seats. I penetrated her again for the second time that night. I remember asking myself

"How in the world is this pussy this good"

I fucked her really hard as she threw that ass back at me. I pulled her hair back and spanked her ass. I fucked her until she screamed "I'm coming" and Right back at her I screamed "me too". I just knew in that moment she was going to change my life. For one, that pussy was just too damn good and that vibe, that connection, that chemistry we had could never be duplicated. She didn't know it yet but, I knew then she was going to be my wife.

(Test number 2 that confirmed she possessed all the qualities of a wife, a life partner)

I was 2 weeks away from taking some vacation days for some much needed time away from work with my lady. I was assigned to a very large parking structure that was experiencing a large volume of vehicle thefts and some theft from vehicles. On that day, I learned to never assume it's going to be an easy day. A few uneventful hours passes and I spotted a male walking from vehicle to vehicle looking through the windows For visible items of value.

I stopped him and asked him if he was lost and he answered no.

I asked him if he had a car parked on the lot and he answered no.

I asked him if he had any forms of ID and he answered no but I have a copy of my last arrest.

I detained him for prowling / unauthorized person on parking lot and upon searching him for that copy of his last arrest, I found a crack pipe and a screw driver. I also found the crumbled copy of his last charge which by pure coincidence was for prowling and again possession of drug related items (aka crack pipe) So, I put the call out to dispatch and requested the transport wagon to transport my buddy to city jail.

All the activity with the police lights must have warned all the working bad guys in the area because it was quiet for a few hours.

But as that good old saying goes. When it rains, it pours.

Another guy walks onto the lot, literally 30 feet from my patrol car and I was in no way trying to hide the car because the mission of the day was to deter crime, not apprehension. This asshole walked onto the lot, completely oblivious to the patrol car looking right at him and began pulling on door handles of parked vehicles. When he realized all the doors were locked, he pulled a metal object from his pocket and was about to break the driver side window.

I jumped out my patrol car and yelled at him "The fuck are you doing"?.

Startled, he looks up and sees the uniform and replies, I didn't do anything and tried to run away but I had already closed the distance between us and grabbed him. He tried to fight but I took him down to the grown and placed the cuff on him. Now I go to stand up and that's when I realized my ankle was broken. I called it out on the air and requested an ambulance from dispatch.

My buddy is trying to get up from the grown so I laid on top of him holding him down until help arrived. I was transported to the hospital where the doctor confirmed I was going to need surgery and now I was more worried about what my girl was going to say because she clearly told me that day to stay away from trouble. (I tend to get into a lot of trouble, in fact they call me the shit magnet).Surprisingly, she came to the hospital concerned rather than upset. Understand something folks, my girl was a sweetheart but when angered.....

(May the good lord bless The Who has forsaken her) let's just say I never wanted to be that guy to piss her off. But to get back on track, she took me to Her mother's house once I was discharged because she did not want me alone. Understand the seriousness of her moving me in with her mother and her 2 girls. She even took time out of work to assure all my medications were in order and my doctor appointments were scheduled. She would leave for work and rush home so she could bathe me, feed me and entertain me because she didn't want me to fall into a depressive state from being home in the bed all day long.

We go through life every single day thinking we have all the time in the world and constantly putting off the things we should have done yesterday. Well life, especially the life I lead as a law enforcement officer is not promised. The cliché of going to work and never returning home is my reality and I don't think I could ever put into words the appreciation I have for this woman for having been there for me in the ways that she has. It gets harder every day and it's written all over my face but how do you live in the moment and ignore the fear of losing the best part of your life.

We entertain people on a regular basis that in no way she or form contribute anything to our lives and there I was with a woman that has shown me Her value, a woman that stands far apart from everyone around her, a woman willing and ready to love me with all my flaws and her focus was on my healing. I remember the day of my surgery, she surely was trying to be strong and not show emotions but I saw the glossy look in her eyes and how hard she was fighting to hold back her tears.

THE ENGAGEMENT

She catered to me hand and foot literally after the surgery. She wanted me to get well enough to go on our trip to Mexico because that trip was already paid for and she made it very clear that we were still going. We somehow managed to make it out to Mexico a week out from surgery with my knee scooter because I on a stricken no weight baring order for the right leg. To make things easier at the airport, the airline rolled me around in a wheelchair so while in Mexico the hotel provided us a wheelchair as well. I have never in my life been a lazy person and was not about to allow this injury to turn me into one. We did everything as we normally would. We worked out at the fully stocked and very impressed gym on the resort. We visited the mall on our first day in Mexico. While at the mall I noticed a jewelry store that specialized in unique diamond rings. I already knew I wanted to ask her to marry me but I wanted to see which type of rings she would gravitate towards while we were there. After she tried on a few rings and sized her finger, I pulled the jeweler to the side and made an arrangement to return the next day and purchased the ring she fell in-love with. We walked around the mall some more and returned to the hotel as the pain was wearing me down.

I now had to come up with a plan on how I would get away from her long enough to return back to the mall. The brain storming was not very productive so I resulted to the number one killer of all relationships. (The cell phone) I came up with the idea of going through her phone and finding something to be mad about. Sure enough I found some old text messages in her phone from even before we started dating. I took that and ran with it by blowing it completely out of proportion. To really get my point across, that night I slept on the couch. I woke up the next morning, jumped in the shower and got in my wheelchair and rolled out (literally, I rolled out).

There I was in a wheelchair rolling through Mexico, not even knowing where I was going but with a vague idea of the route from the bus ride the day before. The shuttle bus was taking too long and I was very eager to get there. I didn't want to be out too long and really fuck things up.

The whole way over to the mall I worried someone else would have gotten the ring and I knew that was the ring she fell in-love with. I rolled myself through the streets in my wheelchair while praying I don't get kidnapped. Let's face it, I really wouldn't be able to defend myself and fight anyone off. I finally made it to the mall after numerous stops to rest my arms.

Have any of you reading this right now ever ridden a wheelchair for an extended period of time in the hot Mexican sun?

That experience has forever changed my level of respect for people in wheelchairs. It surely takes a lot out of you to constantly keep the tire rolling. I made it into the store and to my surprise, the jeweler had already cleaned and set the ring aside anticipating my return. He stated he knew I would return simply by the smile on my face when she tried it on. I called my bank in the US to authorize the amount and made the purchase. Luckily for me the shuttle bus was there By the time I finished because I probably wouldn't have made it back to the hotel. As soon as I made it back to the hotel, I rolled into the event planning office and made reservations for a private dinner on the beach with candle light and rose petals all around the white sandy beach. I notified her mother what had happened and who my plan was she wished me luck with all her blessings. Now made my way back to the room and thinking of how I was going to get her to say yes to dinner after all that had happened. I got to the hotel room and she was in the process of curling her hair. She naturally has beautiful long black hair and I loved nothing more than when she wore it down with a smile. I humbly asked if she would mind attending dinner with me because I had already made the reservation and paid for it ahead of time. She agreed and before she could finish her hair, the down pour began. The hotel sent a bottle of champagne and chocolate covered strawberries to the room along with a message for the change of location. The dinner could no longer be on the beach due to the heavy rain but they planned and decorated a private room along with assigning us a private server. We got dressed and went on down to the lobby and we were met by our private server who escorted us to the private room. The room had rose petals and lit candles all over the floor and on the table. I had already preselected the music for the night when I made the reservation. She still had no idea but she was enjoying the night thus far. When the right song came on, I got up and hopped over to her on one leg and managed to get down on one knee. (It truly was a magical sight to see I promise you). I pulled the ring out of my pocket and her face lit up.

I explained myself and my behavior from the night before and my behavior throughout the day. She could't stop laughing as she warned me "I was gonna kill you". I laughed along with her for a minute but paused as I gathered my thoughts. Looking into her beautiful eyes, I said

"I have been through a lot in my life but never did I think I would end up marrying my best friend. Would you do me the honor of being my wife, will you marry me"?

And without any hesitation she replied "Yes!". I placed the ring on her finger and couldn't help but to cry because I knew she was the one for me from the very first date. We celebrated the night with a tequila fiesta. We had so many shots, we never even opened the bottle of Champaign. I took a million pictures that night and we had so much tequila, we couldn't make it back to the room without getting lost. We laughed so much and so loudly that they could have kicked us out of the resort.

UNBEARABLE

Most of my days are unbearable but somehow,

Today just puts me at my worst because to look at your pictures

And see you with him….

It's not just the picture but the thoughts that come with it.

To know that he has touched you,

Felt you,

And you to him.

I feel so damn broken inside and out.

I have played every scenario out in my head,

In my attempts to make sense of it all.

I just can't understand how you could do this,

After all the things that you've said to me.

Call me stupid but I hung onto your every word.

I wake up every morning thinking this is it,

You have given yourself to another,

You have kissed another

Worst, you have given your heart…

FIRST VDAY

Since you've been gone, I have been dreading this whole entire holiday.

I knew this day would lead me to purgatory.

Today was the longest work day ever..

The wonder of whether or not I crossed your mind.

Last Valentine's, we celebrated together.

Now I was faced with the paralyzing thought of someone else being your valentine.

I have contemplated on a million ways to sabotage any plans you may have but

None of those ways give me you..

Those aware of my pain and anguish say you would have made it clear if you ever

Desired my presence and at the very least, you would have called.

I hope to the high heavens you have not forgotten me.

We truly had a unique connection

I will wait for you.

I will wait until you yourself can stand before me and deny what I know to be your heart's desire

It is not merely as easy to walk away as it is to stand in a crowded room and shout "I love you"

You are not simply another thing that I can just walk away from.

You are the love of my life, I will never give up on that.

I told you that day you walked away.

You took my heart along with you and until you come back

I will remain an empty shell.

A shell just waiting to be whole once again.

I live only where you are & until you come back,

I will just be lost without a heart.

FOR YOU

Today, much like every other day,

I was in a very confused state.

But I am trying to stand firm on my decision

Not to go on any of your social media pages.

Still holding on to hope,

The hope of you coming to your senses.

Hope of you realizing how much I love you.

I find myself making arrangements with myself on

Whether or not to wait until Valentine's Day.

As if it's really going to happen,

Honestly and truly there is no point to which

I wouldn't go for you.

I believe in our love.

Yes, I believe you and I were meant to be.

Whether you believe it or not,

I live in a self-inflicted state of misery every day.

I intentionally seek out music and film that reflect our story.

I have never in my life love anyone the way I love you.

I couldn't deny myself my own truth.

My emotions have been pouring all over the place.

I reflect daily on those moments in which I wish

I could take away all the pain I ever caused you.

Words could never reflect how I regret those moments.

I now wonder if ever you will forgive me

Or will you move on and forget me.

Will you free me from this prison..

Will you take my hand..

Will you make me forever yours..?

JUST ONE

I would give anything,

I would give the world to have one more...

One more smile

One more kiss

One more touch

One more hug

One more night

One more day

One more chance

One more hello

One more goodbye

One more

One more

One more

Just one more.

It's been a while...... but not a day has gone by without you occupying my every thought

Because you are always right here in my heart. I have chosen to keep a little distance

Between us because the Hurt gets greater and greater every time we have to say goodbye.

I've always hated that look in your eyes whenever we had to part.

The last time we were together, I remember you saying "hurry up and fix it so we can be together ".

Those words have played in my head over and over again.

I want to end our pain, as I am certain we are both longing to be together.

I want to be the reason you smile every single day.

I want the next time we are together, to be the very last time we say goodbye.

With your birthday approaching, I have this idea of taking you back on the Brooklyn Bridge

And releasing a balloon for year of celebration.

As you make your birthday wish, we would smash a bottle of Champaign on the iron railing of the bridge.

I just hope your wish matches mine.

Mine is to be the one you celebrate every joyous moment with from this day forward.

I wish to be the one to soak up every tear drop, if ever life should bring you any sorrow.

On days like today, I tend to get this feeling and urge that comes over me.

The urge to simply seek you out wherever you may be and bring you home.

I know the apartment we once shared will never again be home to you,

But Home is where ever we may be together.

We will find our home,

Our sanctuary

But it must start in one another.

Home as in we live in each other's hearts.

People are surviving horrifying circumstances on a daily basis and through all of this, I can

Not think for the life of me what happened that you and I could not have overcome.

Yes, that is the selfish part of me that just wants you to love me and forgive me quicker than I could even say sorry.

That is truly because I have been missing our routine,

But the daily reflections have helped me to understand the importance of patience.

I came across a note you wrote before leaving the house but didn't get to open it until now.

In the note you wrote "I hope you remember me"

Baby, I sleep in the bed every night with every piece of clothing you left behind.

Your scent is still on my pillows.

Your T-shirt is now my pillow case.

Not sure if it's the dreamer in me but, I expected you to know and be assured that I am forever

In thoughts of you as I will forever be in-love with you.

You could never be some estranged person that pops in my head from time to time.

You are and will forever remain the woman I Vowed to spend the rest of my life with,

The woman I have fallen in-love with.

My life, my world is now turned upside down.

All of this should not or Will not be for nothing.

I have noticed Instagram posts of statements like making my actions match my words

But if only you knew.

I am still keeping true to every promise I ever made you.

When you do come back home, I don't want you to ever even have one regret.

PICTURE

What can I say or at least how should I begin

I saw your picture the other day and for 2 straight days, I just wondered.

I decided to take a chance at writing you and to my surprise, I was truly shocked that you even wrote back. We communicated back and forth on small talks but it didn't take long before reflecting on what's happened with us. Now for the lack of a better word you are stuck in my head. When we spoke, the sound of your voice was sooo soothing. I have played the conversation back times and times again. It only makes me want to talk to you even more. But since we are not on a consistent line of communication, I in reaction turn back to that very same picture and stare. As I stare I think back on your choice of musical selections, the movie choices you use to watch while we cuddled in bed (Especially after sex). I remember your curves when you danced for me, I remember your favorite drinks. I now would love the chance to take you out again but not quite sure what it is we would do. . .This distance feels a lot like my life has been taken from me. In fact I wish you had done just that because what you did was taking my heart right out of my chest. To me that is a million times worst. There is nothing greater than loyalty in love and I learned that from you. I have done a lot of hurting to others and I too have been hurt before but it never felt this bad because I simply never loved this strong. The lessons I learned from our relationship bettered me but now what do I do with this betterment. I can't enjoy it with you and not sure if I am willing nor ready to enjoy it with anyone else. I often fantasize about us having one last night to say our peace and goodbyes but then Would it have really made a difference.

Would it have changed the obvious would it have changed the fact of saying goodbye?

I clearly haven't said goodbye because I am constantly writing to you or about you.

Until that moment comes, I will continue to whisper under my breath

Goodbye,

Goodbye.

HOME

This place I use to call home no longer feels like home but

Instead a continent place to rest my head in between shifts.

No more do I look forward to coming home.

Someday home is where The heart is but as of lately

I know not where my heart lies…

But I certainly feel no connection to this place

No connection to the people around me

No connection to those trying to occupy my space and time.

On the inside, I feel captivated, wanting and yearning to be free.

Here I stand calling, screaming for help but no one hears my cry

Do they just not care?

Is this truly my path?

Lord is this cross bears too heavily on my heart

Is it truly the end?

My heart is too sad and broken to accept letting you go

I am truly torn

LEAVING BEHIND

The dream that was once you and I

A distant thought of what once was

What we once thought would last forever

Forever....

How foolish were we

Wishful thinking is what they said...

But having experienced a love like this,

How could I not dream of more

How could I ever be content with the ordinary

No....

I want to dream on..

I want to be rudely awaken

I want to reach out and touch the stars

Please look up...

See the stars..?

Reach out

Reach out with me

Reach out for me

No….?

Guess I'll see you

Around..

DREAMED YOU INTO LIFE

I never imagine this would ever come to be. I can see it as if it was yesterday when I was on a bended knee asking you to marry me

And wanting to spend the rest of my life with you. You owe me explication, how can you imprison my heart this way.?

Tell me all that I have not done. Tell me all that you need me to do. Tell me all that I could be doing and let us make this

Dream a reality once again. I am not nor will I ever be ready to live without you beside me.

Without you as my Queen.

Darling, I don't want you to go. I don't want you to walk away. I don't want to live out the rest of my life in regrets of not making the best love of my life reach its full potential. Since I was a little boy,

I knew to choose you. It started with the idea of finding a lady cop and somehow the universe brought me to

Georgia to find you. I have dreamed you into life.

How can we not be in this moment?

This is blowing my mind. I am here awaiting each day, hoping this day will be the day that you decide to bring our family back together.

The day that you choose us over anything else. The day that we will mark as our new beginning and live out our lives happily ever after.

I Love You. All'll give you my heart. Just have to promise me that you are here to stay way pass forever.

You are my all. My oxygen, my source of life. You are the one for me baby, I see the rest of my life in your eyes.

Recent experience has made me even more aware of just how ready I am for us begin the very best part of our lives.

What will you do with our love?

To know what you truly mean to me you will have to carve my heart open.

You exist & come to life in my every thought, my every wish, and in all my dreams of a future.

I swear to you, I am ready to love you all the way. I am ready to make this dream that I have been dreaming a reality.

This love I have for you will never fade, it will never die out.

I want you to want me the same, I want you to long for us just as bad.

To be near you is electric, I always get this magnetic vibe that just continues to pull me in.

I want you beside me (if not on top of me) all the time. No chains here...

We are all free to do as we want and Somehow, I find my freedom at your feet.

Where ever you are is where I want to be.

My happiness is being in your presence at all times.

I just want to nibble on you to assure that you are real.

You make my head spin with your sexiness, your smile and the way you touch me.

The way your walk changes whenever you know that I am watching.

The way you move when you dance, the way you seduce every bone in my body.

I miss you.

I miss us.

I hate being alone.

I hate being without you.

I truly hate the space between us.

No matter what happens in my life whether it's good or bad, I want you to be the one I share it with.

The one I can't wait to call.

Set my heart free.

Loving you brings out the best in me.

Let me be the man that I know I can be for you baby.

I want us to spend the very best years of our lives building a life worth living.

A life that our kids will look up to, a life they will love and strive for.

I want this love that we share to be the best story of my life.

LOVING HER

I have been loving her for far too long

I am loving her without being her lover

I am alone but never once felt lonely as you are always in my heart.

Deeply in-love with her.

In her absence lies my inability to find happiness

In the presence of everyone else I smile but never happy.

I have chosen to belong only to myself

I will love me as I know she would

I will respect my body as I would respect hers

I will stop wishing and longing for her return

I will now pray that she finds herself and finds love

If the universe ever deems our time to be right, We will somehow meet again as true Loves tend to.

Soulmates will eventually find their way home.

That is the very reason why every single night, I whisper

"Good night my love "and blow a kiss into the wind.

Where ever my love may be, whoever that true love may be

The universe will carry my wish and my kiss to her

As the wind blows....

FACTS

A fact of nature but also a tragedy is that a crown is just an object without being worn

A king is never fulfilled without a Queen.

In meaning I will never be fulfilled without you.

Make me your ultimate desire, let us not allow anything to stand In the way of our love.

You and I are a product of infatuation mangled with passion.

You were once a dream.

The idea of you was but a dream and now a reality.

Reach out to me, take my hand and fear not the unknown.

To be here without you makes me feel like I'm drowning.

I feel as if my chest is caving in.

The anticipation is enough to erupt my heart

I miss you

I want you

No, I need you

DAY AFTER

I woke with a smile on this beautiful day.

As I went through the day, flashbacks of your smile would flash through my head.

I can still feel your touch from holding my hand.

Honestly, I didn't want to let go at all..

So here I stand wishing for you

Wishing for you has reached a boiling point.

I repeatedly reached for my phone to text you but placed it back down.

Finally I gave into my urges but realized I no longer had your number.

You forced me to remove all of your contacts after rudely shutting me down.

Again sadness and sorrow over power me as I struggle with the fact of never recapturing that moment again.

I also struggle with the fact of never seeing you again

But in my mind,

Here in my heart,

Here in this book

Our moment will last forever

SMILING

As I close my eyes,

I can see her smiling.

A smile so damn bright,

You would think the sun was shining.

As she turns to look back at me,

Her energy overwhelmed me.

I knew right at that point I couldn't just capture her heart

But her soul too.

She desired a love that is true

A love filled with purity.

A love truly passionate

A love that should remain timeless even upon the end

As we all know it.

A love that is bound to leave a mark.

A love too rare for the naked mind

WORLDS APART

We are clearly from worlds apart, but none the less we are connected.

We enter this world of confusion with the understanding that there will

Be differences and at times even complications. The age difference

Between us is not significant but it does exist.

It is not at all a problem for me but it may be for you.

If it is, just answer me this question, if we were both cut by the same knife,

Would we not bleed the same??

Would it matter which of us was older?

Would it matter which of us was of a lighter complexion?

With that being said, do not deprive me the pleasure of your smile

Yes, your smile

Your smile is very important to me

I connected with that smile since I first saw it.

I have not forgotten it

Nor has the distance between us broken our connection

Life is all about the paths that we travel

These paths have led us to our first meet

These paths will continue to lead us to our ultimate destination

May it be together or apart…

Some people believe in luck but for me, everything happens for a reason.

To know and understand that reason, you and I will have to continue on

Our journey.

LOST

Today I woke up lost in thoughts of your beautiful smile. I can't begin to tell you just how much I enjoy seeing you with the girls. Even though we are no longer a family, the very first question they asked when they came to visit was to see you. I do hope to enjoy us as a family once again. I don't quite know how to explain this in order for it to make sense but as I think of you, I can actually smell your presence. In case you have forgotten, I absolutely Love your scent. It surely is true that we tend to take things for granted until they are no longer within our grasp. My promise to you is that when you do come back to me, I shall never again take our love lightly. Never again shall I under estimated the value of family and qualify time. I now have this pain in my chest and stomach making it really hard for me to breathe because I am missing you so. If I didn't know any better, I'd think I was going crazy. Every time I walk into the precinct, I look for you and my heart breaks every time because you are nowhere in sight. I look over at your locker and whisper your name.

When you leave your vest out on the chairs, I often would smell it just to feel a little closer to you. I remember your vest being on the chair one evening and a few strings of your hair were hanging on the collar of the vest. So, I picked the hairs off and placed them in my wallet. Ok, even I will admit it was slightly stalker-ish behavior but what other options was I left with. No communication and never saw one another on purpose nor by accident. Embarrassing as these things may sound, they helped me to cope with your absence and certainly with the heartaches.

I at times would even turn on my radio in the daytime hoping to hear your voice because it's the only thing that would bring any kind of relief. I haven't yet told you this but my biggest fear in our entire relationship was to ever let you down and not to live up to the expectations of the man you envisioned. I always planned on getting a Federal position to help provide for you and the girls. I always wanted you to be proud of the man you were about to marry. The rest of our lives should be dedicated to building memories. Everything about you is directly from the woman of my dreams list. I have told you times and times again that a love this strong could never have happened by chance. Through this journey I have learned every love that wonders is not exactly lost. Wondering does something to those of us on the brink of insanity. Insanity is exactly what love is and you've ever truly been there then you too would agree. This love is God's work, this love was intentionally supposed to have been, this Love is the love that songs are written about.

Here on my balcony, I've watched the sun rise and set

Days have come and gone But to you my heart still belong.

SHE AMAZES ME

She simply amazes me… From the corner of my eyes I saw and caught a glimpse of her smile.

It took me back for a few minutes cause I was so darn mesmerized.

I wondered how I could have missed her coming.

She stands out

She is too unique.

So much sexiness that I can't even put in words.

This is just crazy

My heart skipping beats with the thought of her

I can't stay at ease

Constantly wondering if she is wanting me in all the ways that I do her

See her

Feel her

This is something like elementary

I'm having butterflies

Acirfa Valentine

Living in the moment

Wanting to feel her in my arms

Wanting to listen and feel her heart beating

Fantasizing of watching her dance

The seduction motions of her curves

The moment she realizes I'm watching and turns to with a smile

A smile that connects to my core deep within

SLEEPLESS

Last night was another sleepless night.

I tossed, turned and rolled around in the bed so much that I eventually just got up and turned on the TV. Problem is, nothing came on that could keep my mind off you. I then put on my sweats and went for a walk but somehow I ended up in the car driving to your mother's house. I have actually massaged you on those late nights from the front of your house. Sitting there in my car longing to hear the sound of your voice. The sound of your voices travels through me because your voice comes with memories. The sound of your voice has always been able to grace my heart. Something about being there and being so close to you most often turned my night around. This to some may sound like an obsession but what a beautiful obsession to have for the love of your life. To express this obsession a step further I looked forward to work on a daily basis just to be the first to get keys assuring that I was in the same car you were driving that day. Once I got out to the lot I would just sit with my eyes closed for a few minutes to fully take in your scent that was left behind. I would grip the steering wheel firmly as I envisioned your hands and still with my eyes closed, I would whisper your name and tell you that I love you. But getting back on track, I drove back to my house. In the apartment, I played old videos of us together admiring everything about you.

This may sound a bit crazy but if I am crazy in any measure, I am only crazy about you. If it falls under obsession then I am proud to say I am obsessed with loving you. The way I feel when I find myself lost in thoughts of you are very often my happiest moments in the entire day. Those moments can be so electrifying. They always take me on a journey as I visualized the moments of the future that I wish we could have had. In my thick skull, I am still choosing to believe this too will come to pass as our time has not yet expired.

Our time will come around and we will live it to the fullest extent. I had a very long but interesting conversation with my brother-in-law today and his point of view was that

"If she truly is your soulmate, the universe will bring y'all back together"

I was advised to leave you alone which is extremely hard for me. But understanding that nothing I say or do will sway your frame of mind until you yourself are ready. I am choosing to go on faith that love will keep you from falling in the arms of another. I hope to god no other man gets to experience the joy of your sweet loving.

The way you hold me, the way you squeeze me in tightly, the scratches on my back, the freaky dirty words you whisper in my ears when you get lost in the heat of the moment. We all get to that point at time when we begin to wonder what true love really is and whether we would truly give any or everything for it. I am at heart a firm believer in love because through love I have experienced the best as well as the very worst moments of my life. In being true to you, I have to also be honest with you. I regret that day at 3 dollar café. I don't regret telling all there waste really tell but on that day, I regretted not telling you sooner. I know for sure that bit of information played a role in the failure of our

Relationship. I worried about breaking your heart once we were together but understanding your point of view, I broke our circle of honesty and trust. A lot of what has transpired between us has happened because of the broken trust. We had such a beautifully amazing beginning but, at that table you changed. Things between us never went back to being the same. In spite of all my efforts to assure you the divorce was in the hands of the courts, you never saw me or loved me the same. I fully understand that I took away your choice of whether or not you wanted to continue or even start a relationship. The thing is that you always had strong feelings about ever dating a married man and I didn't want to lose my chance at showing you just how serious I was about being with you.

Still it was not my choice to make.

I should have told you that I was still legally separated But Married. You started to show a lot of selfish ways and carelessly did things that would bring me to the conclusions of you possibly out there doing things.

Things that would not at all complement our relationship or commitment.

I should never have to

Life however we choose to live it comes with the choices we make. I made a choice from day one to include you in my life and there for every choice that I have even considered reflected us as a union. I get that we are not yet married but at what point will you stop saying "I" and start to use words like we or Us. For example, everything today was about you. You wanted to eat at Houston's, you then changed your mind to Sweet Auburn. You changed your mind again to Wendy's but the one time I suggested Nagril, you replied "I will go there for lunch tomorrow". As if you are alone, as if you are single. My asking you to stop being selfish, meant just that.

I have and always intended to respect you but at times didn't feel the same coming from you. I am only obligated to my children and our relationship, no one else. Just as you once said that "my time is your time", I expect nothing less from you. If answering to me is too big of a pill to swallow, you truly don't want to marry me because I see nothing wrong with filling you in with whatever it may be that happens in my life.

I have been in relationships where I did my own thing and she did hers. That clearly didn't work out so well and certainly not where I want to be. I have never judged you and I don't plan on starting now so if that is what you want, I will not hold it against you but it will not be with me. I want someone I can spend all my time with, someone I can do everything with. Someone that can read to me as we lay in bed at night, someone that I can work out with, someone that I can explore my sexual fantasies with. When I met you, I prayed that my war with love had finally ended…

But here we are…

Broken

I have been sitting here along the side of the road on I20 where we once made love in the car and I have prayed for you to comeback. I prayed for you to make my life normal once again. I feel like my life is on pause. Every chance I get, I take my guitar out on the balcony and I string along to all the memories. The great laughs, even the many fights we had. When will you come back to lift this heavy burden off my heart. Back to take away the pain, the tears drawn from your absence. I am always taking pictures in the hopes of you seeing them one day. Find myself wondering if the girls ever ask for me, wondering if they will ever come to understand or forgive me for the separation. I know the importance for you to be their role model. I want you to shine as bright as the moon for them. I want to feel the joy of our family again. It makes absolutely no sense the limbo my heart and soul is going through right now so I can only imagine what it's like for the kids. I know if you take the time to look deep within you, beyond the anger, beyond the hurt, you will see that we belong together. You have to open your heart so that you can see just how our love is like no other. My dear love, please don't leave me here to grow old without you. Don't leave me in this misery without your love. Come on back to me, reclaim your thrown. This crown is not meant to fit anyone else baby. It was perfectly sized to you. We are governed by laws in our daily lives, especially in Our profession but right now the law of nature needs to step in.

I will never settle for anything less than greatness…

You have been the greatest love of my life and I could never even imagine anything less.

FOUND

The day we met, I knew exactly what I had found.

I found in you the purpose of dating and the reason for romance. When I found you, I found the courage and the will power to wake up each day. In getting to know who you are and what you went through made me wanna be the man you deserved. The woman I fell in-love with is the reason why even with a broken leg, on crutches, I pushed myself to the limit to turn our apartment into a home. For the woman I fell in-love with I would have laid down my life because when I found you, I knew I had found someone that would reach out with both arms and cater to my every need.

At my moment of weakness, you were my first thought. You were the only one I worried about. I worried about you being mad at me or that I had disappointed you somehow. I didn't even care that my leg was broken in the moment.

Nothing else ever mattered because from the moment I found you, even the sun shined brighter. When its rays touched your skin, you glowed beautifully. My love, you promised you would stay at my side till our dying day.

I know not where I would be at this point had I not found you in time. These days I look for you at every turn.

I look for your traits and habits in everyone I meet. Some have even asked what about you that was so damn special or perfect.

My only reply has been that you weren't perfect but you were perfectly made for me.

You were my perfection..

IMAGINATION

Every single second of the day from the moment I wake to the moment I fall back asleep, I have been in wonders of you.

I work my extra jobs, hit the gym and onto my tour of duty and all the while the memories of us hunt me.

Memories of working extra jobs together, working out together and even you riding with me throughout my tour.

Today the flash backs of our beginning flooded my mind. I was way more fearful than I ever led on. I worried a lot about me overreacting if anything ever happened to you but the more you rode at my side the happier it made me to know that I would always be there for you if anything did happen. I found my sense of security in keeping you safe but most of in knowing that you had my back. You were some kind of a character and truth be told you impressed me most of the time. It's the conversations we shared on those days that help me to fight my fears. It's those conversations that holds me to the belief you would come back someday. In keeping with the belief of your return, I have a daily recurrence of what my first words would be, what the look in my eyes would tell you and what my body language would even look like. The millions of possibilities I play in my head would drive you insane. Throughout the millions of possibilities, I finally have come to a conclusion that would simply be slowly walking up to you kiss you. The power of energy that connects two people is so unbelievably electrifying.

Here I sit writing this down and I can actually feel that connectivity in my veins, in my heart and in even in my lips.

Here I am suddenly warmed and flustered and it is but a thought of you, a thought in my head.

Imagine the actuality of your lips pressing against mine.

To me, nothing else would need be said for that in its own would have said it all.

YOUR EYES

Something about the look in your eyes,

Every single time I look into them, I find myself lost in wonders of you.

The more I look into them, the more they speak to me.

Believe you me, they truly do and what they say I simply cannot put into words.

At times we make connections to others in ways that we cannot explain,

But it doesn't have to end there. It is always up to us to find the reason

To which that connection is based.

Or we can simply watch it pass us by.

The only thing is that once it passes by,

We will forever live with the

"What if"

You my love are my biggest what if

What if the lines weren't blurred?

What if we weren't so damn attached?

123

Acirfa Valentine

What if love just isn't enough?

What if you never loved me as I did you?

What if you and I never met?

What if we weren't meant to be?

What if happily ever after just doesn't exist

Though the journey to our happiness at times may seem like a never

Ending uphill battle, I know for certain this victory is still within our grasp.

Focus not on the masses my darling, for they are but a distraction and you...

You are my destiny.

IN MY HEAD AGAIN

If I could hold you now, just for a little while (no matter how brief that moment should be), it would take away all these lonely nights.

It would at least make the endless wonders worthwhile. There's a famous saying that all things happen in due time but I surely wish time had better timing for us. I at times wonder if this In some way could be my punishment for all the wrongs I have done and The many hearts that I myself have broken.

I have wrongs to make right but this punishment is far too severe.

That entire transition from holding hands one minute to hardly understanding one another is mind blowing. I have fought every single urge whenever I think of finding where ever you may be and in spite of the surrounding, to drop on a bended knee and beg.

If begging should not work, as long as it should lead to your return. But as of lately my wonders have shifted to whether or not we stand to find love on that day.

Time has a way of changing people and it doesn't always work out for the best when 2 hearts that has been parted through heartache reconnect. Most often one half may spend that time on soul searching, meanwhile the other half is left wondering if he or she was ever good enough to begin with. Every now and then I wish you and I could meet and just go over all that has happened and all that we have uncovered about ourselves.

What we have realized of one another.

The only satisfaction that I find these days are in knowing that I actually have tried to reconcile whatever differences that may have stood in the way of our love. Nothing else or should I say no one else has ever gotten close to fulfilling me by far. I have been out to dinners, I have taken trips, I have had sexual encounters and I have even gotten to meet family members of said love interests but sadly through those experiences I always felt empty. Every time I would look over to the other side of me and saw a face that wasn't yours, my excitement in that moment would vanish. Even as I write this, I am envisioning your presence, your smile and the look in your eyes. Calling out your name which at times feel a lot like crying out for you is not at all out of desperation but the realization that I adore you. Can't explain the reasons why I find myself thinking of you whenever I am in the presence of those people crazy enough to find me interesting. I have tried to pretend as much as I possibly could until time ran its course and they all parted. After a while they all noticed the long gaze into thin air, the sadness that would over power me once a slow love song came on the radio. After a while it became too obvious that I was never truly there in the moment and to make matters worse, every social media posting was either in admiration of your love or in fantasies of your return.

In a lifetime, we stand to cross paths with quite a few people that captivates our heart's deepest desire but one of those people will somehow shine just a little brighter than the others. To some it may seem like an obsession.

But to the right one, it will be perfection.

It wasn't too long ago you use to tell me just how much you loved me, these days I can barely get you to text back. Your story has changed to "we need to keep our distance" but love, I can honestly say I don't believe for a second that you have moved on. I just don't know right now where you stand because family and friends have gotten involved. In spite of how many times you said opinions of others will never influence your decision, I have been with you long enough to know better.

The opinions they form of you does matter and most of all you worry about your girls. I beg you to please understand that nothing we do in this life matters to anyone but us. People will forever pass judgement but they will continue to live out their lives and not miss a beat.

Meanwhile you and I are apart, miserable and unfulfilled.

Truth is, in order for love to exist between two people, there has to be a spiritual connection. Without that connection, we are just occupying the same space constantly missing one another. I want something beyond the physical attributes. You have always been the object of my desire. I have never been able to keep my eyes off you. I've always admired the alpha female in you. You have always been very accretive in what you want and need. You have certainly been worthy to be chased and loved. You have always been the "apple of my eye" as they say. Only to you would I ever bare my soul and vice versa. I have always respected and admired the woman that you are but most of all I've admired the way you have always stood out from the rest. There comes true liberations in trusting your love, your heart, your soul in another's hands.

I found that in you my dear love.

YOUR VOICE

I love to hear your sound.

Your sound in all of its magnitudes soothes me like a sweet lullaby

As I press my phone as close as humanly possible to my ear.

Your voice is that musical, that audible vibration which transcends.

Your sound inspires me to create, your sound comforts my inner lonely thoughts.

Your sound even forces me to reflect, as it gives me hope.

Hope of what is to come,

Hope of the many struggles passed were in preparation of your return

I listen to you speak intently

I listen to your rhythm

I listen to your words

You simply captivate my senses

Here I am sipping on my Grand Marnier as I long to hear you once more

Wishing your sound was still in my ear,

Warming my every thought with those sensual overtones

Your sweet sound resonates deep in my heart

The articulations

The subtle amplitudes.

Every utterance brings a sense of fulfillment,

A sense of satisfaction,

A craving to hold you closely in my arms and to

Just

Listen.

BETTER DAYS

Have I ever really had any...

I can think of days before you came along and those days weren't necessary better but waking up out of bed was certainly easier. In those days, life was boring on a day to day basis. The best part of my day then was looking forward to the gym and the amount of arrest I was going to make that day. Those days were simply a different kind of worry.

My worry was more so of what my meal prep would be for the week but these days I find it hard to breathe.

The pain believe it or not is interesting. There is something to be said out pain and suffering.

In spite of the many ups and downs, I am grateful for the Journey. There is absolutely nothing more satisfying than the pleasure of getting to know someone whole heartedly. The journey of discovery. The journey of 2 complete strangers becoming one.

Becoming one in terms of viewpoints, becoming one as their emotional connection grows and as they physically adopt to one another's way of life.

It is said that to live in the past means that you are dead in the present but I don't agree. Not in every situation but in some cases, reliving the past leads to the future. Whether it means to right the wrongs, getting a second chance or simply accepting your flaws and making the necessary changes for the next love to journey.

Happy or sad we all change one another after a break up. Some change for the best when others choose to never be vulnerable again.

Vulnerability allows us that space to discover love and love is an entirely different concept to each and every one of us. The only absolute certainty we have in life is the fact that no two people are alike. That whole new discovery with each person and an entirely new set of memories created. Memories help to strengthen if not stitching together the broken pieces of our hearts.

I vow to always remain in a positive frame of mind though the journey to find the love made for me. The moment we allow our experiences to change our energy, the makeup of our DNA and just that easily, the path of our journey can then also change. As we now begin to attract the same energy we project onto the world. Love is not by any means a safe playground and most certainly will leave each and every last one of us scarred.

Days before you, I worried of succeeding in the career path which I have chosen but these days I focus solely on writing of past memories.

The days before you I longed for love only to now realize that you are that love.

Love is my journey.

LOVE

What is Love?

Is it that excruciating pain that hunts me when you are no longer here at my side.

My conflicted state of mind cannot conform to the normalcy of your absence.

Is it the awakening of uncertainties, because loving you was so much easier once

Upon a time but this hurt I feel continues to linger on.

Is it the guarantees of a successful relationship which we so whole heartedly wish we could

Grasp

Because to know that another has had the other half of me fuels me up with a sense

Of resentment.

Is it the overcoming of our worries or fears of reoccurrences from our past

Because the trauma of heartbreaks passed continue to weigh heavily on our minds.

Again I ask,

What is Love?

Because every time I think I'm gaining grounds

Every time I feel it's within my grasp,

It vanishes.

IMAGES

These days I find less pleasure in these photographs that I've been holding onto so dearly. I am now at the point where I don't even look at them anymore but somehow the difficulty to delete them hasn't gotten any easier. These days I find myself looking in the mirror asking how this woman can have such a strong hold on me. How can she have me this discombobulated? I struggle daily with this hold that you have on me. As I struggle with this phenomenon, I tend to ignore all the women that fight for my attention or even my body but sex is of no interest to me. I care not even one bit to entertain any of them. I often find myself telling them about you as they all try to point out the wrongs or flaws in you. Some of them actually made sense but still here I am stuck on you. Stuck on the memories of you I should say. Stuck on the moments that made us great. Nothing you have done and certainly nothing anyone says will ever change the way I looked at you.

The vision I saw when I laid eyes on you.

So, here I am tonight deleting and destroying images of you, images of us. How can this be so damn difficult, I am ready to move forward and become the version of me with all the lessons learned from loving you.

Tonight I deleted the images and videos of you and before the confusion of what if comes over me all over again. I need not to look back anymore after your last statement of

"I want no part of whatever you have going"

I need no more remembrance of what was.

In the words of Will Smith, "we must embrace failure for it is our greatest teacher". So, let us fail forward as we better ourselves.

MY DEAR J

I've been going back and forth for the past few days debating if I should write this. I realized I would most certainly regret it if I didn't.

The last time we saw each other, we weren't exactly whispering sweet nothings in each other's ears. I remember telling you that my reality was that I may never get over you and you replied with the song by Sam Smith "too good at saying goodbye".

It certainly wasn't the way I wanted that day to go. I suppose I can be blamed for that one. I did ask you to relocate and start fresh, because in all honesty, if given the chance I would do it all again.

You once said I was no longer the man you fell in-love with. There Is no way I can trace back that man but I can be me.

The person I am today and that is the best version of me. So, I would rather you get to know and love this man here today.

I have grown stronger and wiser after all that we have been through. If ever we could find that joy and happiness that would help us heal and move forward. You always said you were not like everyone else and that has proven to be true. You are truly one of a kind my love.

I once heard a quote "our lives are streams flowing into the same river towards whatever heaven lies in the mist beyond the falls".

My dear love, I hope and pray the waves of life finds you some happiness.

The kind that I was not able to give you.

You truly are my happiness.

I look back and I regret nothing because you made me whole. You were my slice of heaven here on earth.

I will forever want you

Forever miss you

Forever love you

Today is a new day and I want to grab the bull by the horns. I am no longer at the place where I needed to be convinced.

I am no longer hanging onto "what ifs". I am at the top of the mountain. I have shared my testimony over and over again with whoever was still willing to listen. I am now talked out. I am even cried out. Yes, I said cried out. The idea of a grown man shedding tears over a love lost may sound emasculated but trust & believe these tears have been more therapeutic than anyone I have ever spoken to.

These tears have transformed me and made me realize my own vulnerability. Our vulnerabilities allow us the space to look deep within ourselves and look at the dark secrets that we stashed away in order to never be judged. My new favorite quote now is "let he who is without sin cast the first stone" which has now made me stronger than ever before. I am finding the good in this heartbreak, in hopes that it will be my last.

This love has not at all jaded my optimism in finding the one meant for me. I had a talk with my mother and her exact words were "the one meant for you will be the one to pull you up and guide you to your true greatness because her strength will be somewhat of an angel".

She will love me so unconditionally that I will never again look back in wonder, never will I need to apologize nor will I ever again have the need for validation. The daily expressions will be that of to the moon and back.

A love till the end of time, a love that reveals itself in ways that need not be explained.

CONFLICTED

Have you ever gotten to a point in life where you were conflicted on what direction you should go.

When your issues vary from relationships, career choices or anything that may be life altering.

The answer to these issues can be answered if we remember to trust in God and let him lead our way.

Let me tell you a thing or 2 about god.

God has been in the business of leading us since he lead the Israelites out of Egypt.

During those days, God led the people through the way of the wilderness of the Red Sea (Exodus 13:21).

Try following the cloud and fire and you will be in your rightful place.

Often times we question why our lives don't go the way we plan, without realizing that we times get in the way of God's plan

We do not let God do his work for our lives. We may have to go through hell for God to get us to our Heavenly place.

Trust in the Lord with all your heart and lean not on your own understanding.

In all your ways submit to him, and he will make your paths straighter than you could even imagine.

Being patient and waiting on God is a sure way to happiness.

Do not allow the stressors of life to overtake the will of the father.

Instead, remove yourself from the center of things & allow God to be the center.

He is more equip & will get desired results in a shorter time frame without the added stress to you.

He knew you before the beginning of time. As a result, He paved a path of success specifically for you.

Submit & accept his way & he will guide you to a victory

DEAR PAST

Today is the very last time I will write to you.

Last time I even write about you.

I know not where I will end up by the time you get to read this but I surely hope that life has been good to you.

Life is in fact a roller coaster as they say. You and I got on and managed to hold on tightly through

The ups and downs. Leaving us here right back where we started, apart as 2 strangers.

Proving once again the only thing as certain in this life as death and taxes

Is the fact that whatever once was Will one day again return.

Life is funny that way.

Even though reincarnation is a belief shared by a large portion of the world's population,

I must make peace in knowing that we may not be so lucky.

All that you promised me sounded so damn good but sadly not the hand I was dealt.

I so truly enjoyed all our times but looking back, I just know the bad may weigh too heavily been

Too much for a person to let go of and possibly forget.

I certainly am happy the person I was with you has come to pass.

I have given you entirely too much credit over my present and with

That I bid you the very best of luck in all that you touch, it just will never again be me that you touch.

Mistakes are made for a reason, they are made so that we learn through them.

It's been heavenly knowing your kind of love

But......

I hope to live a much better life in my next go round.

Printed in the United States
By Bookmasters